Foundation

GCSE
Citizenship Studies
for AQA

Joan Campbell • Sue Patrick

Heinemann Educational Publishers
Halley Court, Jordan Hill, Oxford, OX2 8EJ
Part of Harcourt Education

Heinemann is a registered trademark of
Harcourt Education Limited

© 2003 Joan Campbell, Sue Patrick

First published 2003

06 05 04 03
10 9 8 7 6 5 4 3 2 1

ISBN 0 435 80817 6

British Library Cataloguing in Publication Data is available
from the British Library on request.

Edited by Phebe Kynaston

Designed by Bridge Creative Services Limited

Typeset and illustrated by Bridge Creative Services Limited

Printed and bound in Spain by Edelvives

Acknowledgements
The publishers would like to thank the following for permission to reproduce copyright material:

Maps and extracts
p. 11 *The Guardian*, Clare Dyer, 20 March 2002; **p. 26** 1.5, 1.6 *Kick it Out*, October 2001; **p. 40** Nissan Motor Manufacturing (UK) Ltd; **p. 57** *Observer*, Neasa MacErlean, 24 February 2002; **p. 102** *Daily Mirror*, 11 March 2002; **p. 102** *Daily Mirror*, Voice of the Mirror' 13 March 2002; **p. 104** *Daily Mirror*, James Hardy 16 March 2002; **p. 105** *Guardian*, Ian Black, 16 March 2002; **p. 109** Christian Aid; **p. 109** *The Guardian*, John Pilger, 4 March 2002; **p. 133** Greenpeace; **p. 133** *The Times*, Robert Whyman, 23 March 2002.

Photographs
pp. 7, 18 Ace Photoagency **p. 54** Ace Photoagency /John Searle **p. 77** Ace Photoagency/ Roger Howard **p. 38** Acestock/Chris Middlebrook **p. 35** Alamy/Peter Bowater **p. 60** AP Photo/Jeff Widener **p. 25** Commission for Racial Equality **p. 97** Corbis/Ric Ergenbright **p. 26, 150** Empics/Matthew Ashton **p. 26** Empics/Neal Simpson **p. 131, 132** Greenpeace **p. 71** Hulton Archive **p. 125** Impact Photos **p. 43** Impact Photos /Peter Arkell **p. 45** Impact/Alain Evrard **p. 117, 108** Impact/Alan Kedhane **p. 102** Impact/Brian Harris **p. 80** Impact/Bruce Stephens **p. 141** Impact/Mark Henley **p. 46** Impact/Martin Black **p. 129** Impact/Mike McQueen **p. 88** Impact/Peter Arkell **p. 62, 60** Impact/Petteri Kokkonen **p. 59, 72** Impact/Piers Cavendish **p. 45** Impact/Robin Lawrence **p. 142** Impact/Rupert Eames **p. 46, 143** Impact/Simon Shepheard **p. 31** Impact/Tony Page **p. 8, 13, 23, 27** John Walmsley **p. 86** Network/ Christopher Pillitz **p. 116, 108** Network/Anthony Suau **p. 85, 150** Network/Barry Lewis **p. 110, 138** Network/Gideon Mendel **p. 82** Network/Jonathan Olley **p. 56, 4** Network/Justin Leighton **p. 149** Network/Martin Mayer **p. 53, 127** Network/Mike Goldwater **p. 39** Nissan Motor Manufacturing (UK) Ltd **p. 36** Photodisc **p. 19** Photofusion/Bob Watkins **pp. 10, 15, 34, 41, 55, 56, 65, 74, 77, 81, 98, 107, 109, 117, 124, 129, 140, 150** Popperfoto **p. 15** Popperfoto/Paul Bates/Reuters **pp. 4, 15, 60, 63, 93, 99, 104, 119** Popperfoto/Reuters **pp. 4, 29, 37, 45, 52, 53, 60, 61, 68, 69, 91, 111, 112, 122, 137, 145** Rex Features **p. 15** Rex Features/ Michael Powell **p. 76** Rex Features/ Simon Walker **p. 101, 60** Rex Features/Brian Rasic **p. 113, 4** Rex Features/SIPA **p. 19** Rex Features/Tim Rooke **p. 66** Robert Harding/ Adam Woolfitt **p. 47** Robert Harding/Adina Tovy **pp. 30,114** Roger Scruton **pp. 4, 8, 12, 14, 17, 24, 48, 49, 73, 80, 83, 84, 90, 135, 150** Sally & Richard Greenhill **pp. 8,11, 15** Sipa Press/Rex Features **p. 108** SPL **p. 144** SPL/Ted Kerasote **pp. 60, 100, 108, 126, 139** Still Pictures **p. 42** Still Pictures/ Klaus Andrews **p. 134** Still Pictures/Mark Edwards

The publishers have made every effort to trace the copyright holders, but if they have inadvertently overlooked any, they will be pleased to make the necessary arrangements at the first opportunity.

Picture research by Thelma Gilbert

Websites
On pages where you are asked to go to www.heinemann.co.uk/hotlinks to complete a task or download information, please insert the code **8176P** at the website.

Tel: 01865 888058 www.heinemann.co.uk

Contents

Introduction

Studying to become a good citizen

This book aims to help you with the GCSE Short Course in Citizenship Studies. You should think carefully about things that happen in your local community as well as national, European and global issues so you can make your own opinions on each issue. The course has three main topics:

- **Topic 1**: School, work and the local Community
- **Topic 2**: National and European citizenship
- **Topic 3**: Global citizenship.

In addition, the course has three themes:

- **Theme 1**: Rights and responsibilities
- **Theme 2**: Decision-making, power and authority
- **Theme 3**: Participation in citizenship activities.

To do well with this course, you must:

- do the research needed
- talk about issues in pairs and in groups
- take part in role-play activities
- use books, the Internet and CD ROMs
- take part in school and community activities.

What are the values you need?

For yourself, you need to have good self-esteem and take responsibility for yourself.

In your relationships with others, you need to:

- value others for themselves
- respect other people whatever their age, religion, sex or culture
- be loyal and trustworthy

- be able to work with others
- be able to sort out differences without violence.

As a member of society, you need to:

- value truth and justice
- respect a person's human rights
- act reponsibly
- respect the law
- encourage equal opportunity for all
- help those who are unable to help themselves.

As a global citizen, you should support sustainable developments to save the planet's resources for the future, understand your responsibilities to other nations and their peoples and help to protect plants and animals.

Developing personal skills

Building confidence

Be confident about yourself and do your best. Don't say that you can't do something. Know when to apologize for a mistake. Don't let your peers' comments put you down.

To raise your confidence you should be:

- positive – think about issues carefully and look at life in a positive way
- true to yourself – think about an issue and make up your own mind about how you feel about it
- realistic – set yourself reasonable targets that you can achieve with hard work
- accepting – accept the point of view of others. If you are wrong, learn to apologize. This is not a sign of weakness

- brave – have a go at new things. Even if they don't work, you'll know that you've tried. If they do work, it will give your confidence a boost!

Believing in yourself

Have a good opinion of yourself, know what your strengths are and use them. Good self-esteem will:

- make you feel confident in your thoughts and actions

- allow you to take risks and try new experiences

- help you believe in your own judgements

- help you get on with other people

- help you to express your opinion openly

- help you accept that others may hold a different opinion to you.

Developing communication skills

Forming your own opinion

An opinion is a statement based on a particular point of view or on a feeling or belief. A fact is a true statement that has been experienced or observed.

Before you take part in a discussion or debate:

- find out the facts – research your facts in books, articles and on the Internet

- note the arguments for and against the issue and identify the main points

- decide what your opinion is and make notes of the reasons why you hold that opinion.

Taking part in role-play situations

Role play allows you to think about someone else's views by standing in their shoes. In a role play you must become that person and act out your role in a way that is faithful to your new character. You should think about:

- how the person you are playing would act

- what they would say

- how they would think in certain situations.

Developing research and writing skills

Active research and case studies

Throughout this course you will need to spend time looking at information to answer questions relating to your citizenship studies. Try to keep notes of your research for future reference. Use the case studies to explore your feelings about situations and issues that need you to think and act like a good citizen.

Developing your writing skills

Throughout your time at school you have been developing your skills as a writer. In this course you should develop your own style of writing as you express your own views and feelings. To write an essay or report, you should:

- research your topic carefully

- make notes about the main facts and sources of your information

- make a plan listing all the points you want to include

- state your opinion clearly in the opening paragraph, giving your reasons

- give examples to support your statements

- end your writing with a statement which sums up your views and ideas.

When you have finished your piece of writing ask yourself the following questions:

- Does it have a good opening?

- Are the main points supported by evidence?

- Does the writing keep the reader interested?

- Does it have an appropriate ending?

If the answer to all of these questions is yes, then you have produced a good piece of writing.

School, work and the local community

Key ideas

Chapter 1 School

* Rights and responsibilities
* Rights and responsibilities of children, parents, teachers and pupils
* Power and authority
* The school community
* The local community
* Equal opportunities

Chapter 2 Work

* Rights and responsibilities of employers and employees
* Health and safety
* The economy
* How do businesses use financial services
* Money matters – you and your money
* Types of business
* Industry sectors
* Work experience

Chapter 3 Local community

* Community life
* Local government
* Devolution – regional government in the UK
* Voting systems
* How individuals can bring about change

What rights and responsibilities, do you think, are being demonstrated in these photos?

He fought, peaceably, for equal rights for black people. Sometimes fighting for your rights takes years of patient work.

What is work? Is it still work if you don't get paid for it? Do street corner musicians work?

1 School

Rights and responsibilities

Rights and responsibilities is one of three themes that we will talk about throughout this course. We have many different parts to play during our lifetime: child, teenager, pupil, student, parent, employee, motorist and shopper. In each of these we have different rights and responsibilities.

Legal and moral rights and responsibilities

Legal rights and responsibilities are what we can and can't do according to the laws of the land. For example, every child has the legal right to be educated.

Moral rights and responsibilities are what is generally expected of normal decent people leading ordinary lives, as most of us do. For example, parents have the moral responsibility to care for their children. We can also describe moral rights and responsibilities as what we are expected to do according to the values of the society we live in.

The **values** of society are the things that are considered to be good and worthwhile. They include a code of behaviour, which is the way we are expected to behave.

Human rights

After World War II a group of nations formed the Council of Europe. They drew up a charter, or agreement, to protect human rights. This is referred to as the European Convention on Human Rights, or the ECHR.

The convention guarantees citizens of all the countries that have signed and agreed to it (ratified the convention) sixteen basic human rights. These include the right to:

- liberty
- justice
- privacy

- education
- freedom of thought and expression
- freedom from slavery and forced labour (work).

The European Court of Human Rights in Strasbourg protects these rights. If a person thinks that their government (not a company or another person) has affected these rights, they can appeal to this court. You can see the court in session in the picture below. The court is usually a panel (or chamber) of nine judges, but for really difficult cases there may be 21 judges. They listen to all the evidence and reach a decision. Their decision is final and there is no appeal.

The United Kingdom (UK) was one of the original members of the Council of Europe, and signed the convention. However, it was not until 1998 that Parliament passed a law on human rights. This is known as the Human Rights Act 1998. The Act sets out how the rights under the convention are now applied to all British laws.

This means that claims can now be heard in British courts, and people do not have to take their case to Strasbourg. However, some people may still wish to do so, as in the case study on page 11.

European judges in the Grand Chamber

Activities

1 Make a list of all the different groups that you belong to, for example family, youth club, sports team.

2 Copy and complete the table below. Add another group you belong to in the column on the right. Write in all the rights and responsibilities you can think of. Some have been included to get you started.

	Family	School	
Rights	To be cared for	To be educated	
Responsibilities	To help around the house	To go to school regularly and on time	

Your rights under the Human Rights Act 1998 are taken from the following articles and protocols:

Article 2	Right to life
Article 3	Prohibition of torture
Article 4	Prohibition of slavery and forced labour
Article 5	Right to liberty and security
Article 6	Right to a fair trial
Article 7	Punishment must be lawful
Article 8	Right to respect for private and family life
Article 9	Freedom of thought and religion

Article 10	Freedom of speech
Article 12	Right to marry
Article 14	Prohibition of discrimination
Article 17	Prohibition of abuse of rights
Article 1 of Protocol 1	Protection of property
Article 2 of Protocol 1	Right to education
Article 3 of Protocol 1	Right to free elections
Article 1 and 2 of Protocol 6	Abolition of the death penalty

Case study

Diane Pretty makes final 'death with dignity' plea

Clare Dyer, legal correspondent, Guardian

WEDNESDAY 20 MARCH, 2002

Diane Pretty, the terminally ill woman who wants her husband to be allowed to help her commit suicide, made a final plea for the right to die with dignity at the European court of human rights yesterday.

The bench of seven judges in Strasbourg is Mrs Pretty's last hope after her plea was rejected by the high court, the court of appeal, and the House of Lords.

Paralysed from the neck down by motor neurone disease and with only months to live, she insisted on making the 12 hour journey from her home in Luton, Bedfordshire, through the Channel tunnel in a private ambulance with paramedics and an intensive care nurse in attendance ...

She listened intently as her QC, Philip Havers, argued that her 45-year-old husband should be allowed to help her take her life without fear of prosecution.

After the hearing Mrs Pretty, 43, who can speak only with the help of a voice synthesizer, said: 'I just want my rights.' ...

Jonathan Crow, representing the government, expressed sympathy for the 'tragic circumstances' of Mrs Pretty's case but said the law on assisted suicide was clear ...

The judges are expected to give their ruling within weeks.

Taken from the *Guardian*, 20 March 2002. (Mrs Pretty died in a hospice on 11 May 2002.)

(A) Activities

Read the case study and talk about the following questions.

1 Why did Mrs Pretty take her case to Strasbourg?

2 Which human right did Mrs Pretty base her claim on?

3 Do you think there is ever a case for euthanasia? Give reasons for your answer.

Rights and responsibilities of children, parents, teachers and pupils

A right is something we are all entitled to. Rights are sometimes called entitlements or freedoms.

Sometimes one person's right may be another person's responsibility. For example, a child has a right to love and care, which is usually the responsibility of the parents.

Children's rights

Children rely on their parents to protect and care for them. In many parts of the world children's rights are being abused. Some children work many hours a day in poor conditions for very low wages.

In 1989 the United Nations drew up a Convention on the Rights of the Child. This became part of international law in 1992 when twenty different countries signed and agreed to it.

This convention tries to protect children's rights all over the world. The basic rights it sets out are for:

- food, health and a decent place to live
- free education and information
- freedom of thought
- protection from slavery, exploitation and cruelty
- freedom for children to give their opinions on issues which affect them.

The rights of children in the United Kingdom (UK) are covered by the Children Act 1989. This Act of Parliament puts the well-being of the child above everything else. It is now the law that in certain situations the view of the child must be taken into account.

Children's responsibilities

As a child grows up, the rights begin to have more responsibilities attached to them. For example, the right to education brings with it the responsibility to go to school regularly.

As children reach certain ages they are allowed, by law, to become more and more responsible for their own actions. You will find a list of what you can do at different ages on page 79.

Family time – eating a meal together

Parent's rights and responsibilities

Parents have the right to:

- free education for their children from the age of five to sixteen

- choose the school they want their children to go to

- decide which religion their children are brought up in

- decide on discipline and punishment – this does not mean physical abuse

- choose medical treatment for their children.

Parents are responsible for the health, care and control of their children until the children reach the age of eighteen. This means that parents make sure that their children:

- have a home to live in

- are fed, clothed and cared for

- receive proper medical treatment when they are ill

- attend school regularly

- behave in a reasonable manner

- know right from wrong.

If married parents separate or divorce and they cannot agree about the care of their children, then a court will decide. This court has many powers and will consider all the details of each case it judges very carefully. The main concern is what is best for the children, taking into account the age and wishes of the children.

Rights and responsibilities of pupils

The Education Act 1997 introduced home–school agreements. Parents are usually asked to sign a home–school agreement when a child starts a new school. This agreement sets out what is expected of everyone involved.

A pupil is a person under the age of nineteen who still goes to school. A student is a person who is in full-time further education at a college or in higher education at a university.

Pupils have the right to:

- a safe place to learn

- good teaching

- be told how they are getting on and how they can improve.

Pupils helping each other to learn new skills

Pupils have the responsibility to:

- go to school regularly and on time
- behave reasonably and follow the school rules
- make sure they have what they need for lessons
- work hard – do their best
- respect other people – both pupils and teachers.

Rights and responsibilities of teachers

While pupils are in school, teachers act 'in loco parentis' – this simply means in place of parents. They make sure that pupils are in a safe place where they can learn.

The main responsibilities of teachers are to:

- keep up to date with their own subject
- teach well
- make their classroom interesting
- help and encourage pupils to learn
- mark work and show pupils how they can do better
- tell pupils and parents what progress is being made
- notice any problems with learning.

Teachers have the right to:

- a safe place to work
- expect pupils to behave well and do their best
- further training when needed, for example to keep up to date.

Teacher and pupils working together

A Activities

1 Do you think all the people who make up a school community have the same right to trust and respect from each other? Why?

2 Pages 12–14 outline some of the most important rights and responsibilities of children, parents, teachers and pupils. What other rights or responsibilities do you think are important? Talk about your opinions with other members of your group.

3 Draw a table like the one below. Fill in the rights and responsibilities using the information and results from your discussions.

	Rights	Responsibilities
Pupils		
Parents		
Teachers		

Power and authority

(i) What is power? What is authority?

Power means being able to influence or to rule. Power may be held by a group of people, or just one person. We say that the government is in power. The government influences what happens in the country, and makes decisions and changes.

Authority is a form of power. In a democracy people accept that the representatives they elect to Parliament have the authority to make laws. These laws then have to be followed by all the people.

Coercion means rule by force. Dictators rule by coercion – they do not offer people any choice.

Nelson Mandela

There are three types of authority:

- **Legal authority** means that people obey the law because we need to have peace and order in our society. People accept a person's authority because of their position, for example a police officer.

- **Charismatic authority** comes from the very strong personal qualities of an individual. Such people can bring about change. For example, Martin Luther King was a black civil rights leader in the USA in the 1960s and led a peaceful campaign for black rights.

- **Traditional authority** is based on traditions that have been built up over many years. In this case we accept the authority because it is our custom, for example the monarchy.

Police officers

The Queen

Osama bin Laden

Tony Blair

Activity

A

Look at the photographs on pages 15 and 16. Decide which of the following types of authority each of these people has:

- legal
- charismatic
- traditional.

Who has power and authority in schools?

Economic power

The people who provide the money or funding have power. The money for schools comes from the local council. Local councils receive money in two ways:

- from government grants
- from the council tax.

Education is one of the major costs to any council. The council gives each school a set amount of money (a budget). The school governors and the head teacher are responsible for this money. They have the power to decide how the money should be spent.

Pupil power

Pupils of the same age will form friendship groups with others who have similar interests. This is known as a peer group. Peer groups have a very big influence on the individual members of the group.

Think about your group of friends – your peer group. Who are the members of the group? Are you all about the same age? Do you have the same interests?

Do your friends affect some of the choices you make about:

- the kind of music you listen to
- the type of clothes you wear
- what you do in your free time
- your attitude towards school?

The bullies are individuals or small groups who try to use coercion to get what they want. Every school will have ways of dealing with bullying and will try to prevent it happening.

In some schools there are year councils or school councils. Pupils are elected and then present the opinions of their group at meetings. From the discussions at these meetings some changes may be made to school life.

 Activity

Talk about whether you think school councils are a good idea. Give reasons for your view.

Walking to school together

Parent power

Parents use the power of choice when they choose a school for their children.

Parents also elect people to represent their view on the governing body of the school.

School governors

The Education Reform Act 1988 says what school governors are responsible for.

They have the power to run the school, but they have to follow the regulations that the local council set out. These regulations are known as the Instruments of Government of a school.

Head teachers

The head teacher is the representative of the governors in the school. The head teacher is responsible for the daily running of the school.

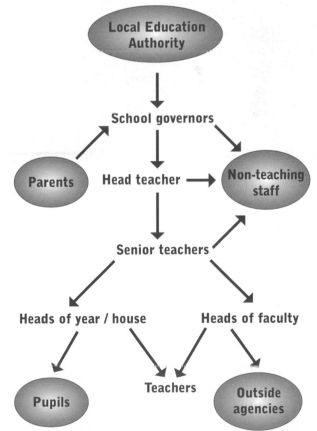
Figure 1.1 Who has power in schools?

The school community

Each school is a small community. Lots of people work together, follow the same set of rules and share similar values.

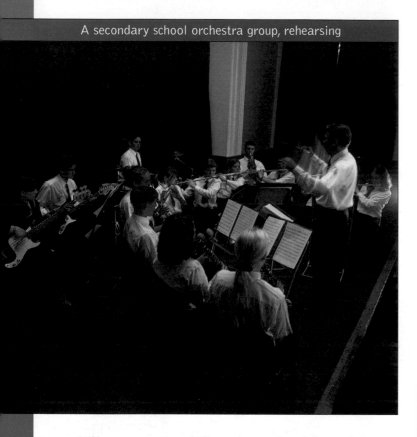

A secondary school orchestra group, rehearsing

There are many different people who work in a school, as well as pupils and teachers, who make up the school community. Each person has their own job to do, and all of them are important. Some of the people in the school community are secretaries, caretakers and cleaning staff. How many others can you think of?

In school there will be many ways in which you learn about becoming a responsible adult.

You may be given a special task to do in your form, such as collecting or returning the register, or collecting homework and taking it to a teacher. You may help with refreshments at parents' evenings or be involved with a school play or concert. In all these you give your time and effort to help the school community.

Taking responsibility for simple tasks and being relied on to complete the task is important. Your efforts will be noticed and appreciated. As you become an adult you will find that these qualities (characteristics) are very important in the wider community and the world of work.

Many schools encourage pupils to learn about the democratic process (how we elect people to represent us) by holding elections for year councils or school councils. This gives pupils experience of elections. It also gives those who are elected the responsibility of speaking at meetings on behalf of the pupils who elected them.

Most schools will have rules that everyone is expected to follow. This is so that all members of the school community know what is expected of them. They will also be told what happens if the rules are broken.

Most schools have just a few simple rules.

(A) Activities

1 Think about the tasks you have been asked to do at school and answer the following questions:
   - Who have you helped?
   - Did you complete the task?
   - Did you enjoy the responsibility?
   - Did you do the task willingly?

2 Write down:
   - two other tasks you might do to help your teachers
   - two other tasks to help the school.

3 a Make a list of all the different activities and clubs at your school.

   b Tick the ones you belong to.

Figure 1.2

When these are followed, life is a lot easier for everyone in the school community.

 Activities

1 Ask your head teacher or a senior member of staff to come to talk to your group about why the school has rules. Then ask them about:

- who is responsible for making the school rules

- who is responsible for making sure the school rules are followed.

2 Talk about why school rules are important.

3 What do you think would happen if there were no school rules?

The school and the wider community

When a school invites local people to take part in an event, such as coming to a summer fair or to watch a school play, there is a feeling of belonging to a much wider community.

A fund-raising or charity event, such as Children in Need, can be an important way of involving the wider local community.

The Children in Need events take place all over the country every November. This can be a lot of fun for everyone and many children benefit from the money raised.

Red Nose Day is another similar popular event.

Organizing and taking part in a fund-raising event could be your coursework project. This would need a lot of discussion and planning with your teacher before it could go ahead.

A school summer fair

Children in Need's Pudsey Bear

- Within your group, decide who will do each job. Remember each member of the group has to make a contribution.

- Plan what has to be done and by when. You could write this out as a chart.

- Talk about your plans with your teacher. Is there anyone else you need to talk to?

- Make any changes to your plans.

- Carry out your plans.

- Write up your own account of what you did. This should include:

  - your plans showing the jobs each person was set and when they had to be completed by – this could be a chart

  - how successful the event was – think about your contribution and that of the others in the group

  - who benefited from the activity

  - how much you raised

  - whether you enjoyed the activity – why/why not?

Organizing a fund-raising activity

For this to be successful you need to work with people you can rely on to do their share of the work.

This will involve a lot of thought, very careful planning and a lot of discussion.

- Begin by making a list of activities that you could actually do in the time allowed.

- Talk about your ideas as a group and make a decision.

- Talk to your teacher about the ideas and be guided by the advice given.

(A) Activities

1 Think about all the people who work in your school. Find out more about the responsibilities of one or two people.

2 In small groups, make a list of fund-raising activities you could organize.

3 Think about :

- what makes your school a community?

- how is your school involved with the local community?

- is your school democratic?

The local community

Where are U in your commUnity?

A community is made up of all the people who live in an area, as well as all the facilities and services in that area.

Facilities are things like parks, swimming pools, leisure centres and cinemas. Services include schools, libraries, play groups, dentists, doctors, the police and fire brigade.

Some communities will have different buildings, houses, services and facilities from other communities. The differences usually depend on where the community is. A community in a town or city is known as an urban community. A community in the countryside is known as a rural community. People within a community may organize or join local groups providing leisure, sport or educational activities, for example a parent and toddler group, a five-a-side football team or a lunch club for older people.

Some community schools provide a range of courses and leisure activities for people of all ages. Some adults join in AS or GNVQ courses at some schools.

(A) Activity

Look at the ideas web below and talk about which services, buildings and types of people are found in your own community.

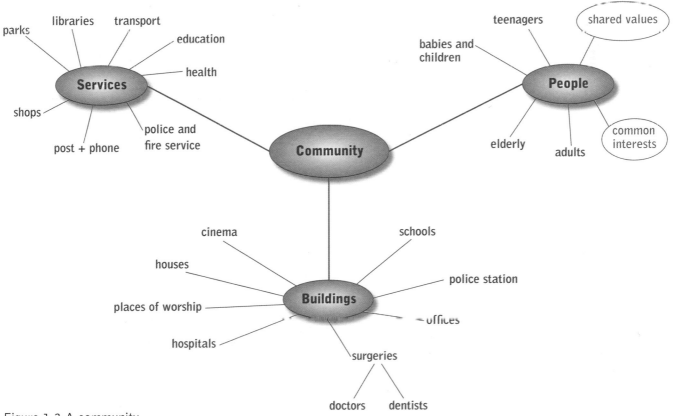

Figure 1.3 A community

Case study: The community and you

 Activities

Read the case study and talk about the following questions:

- Do the teenagers mean to disturb Mrs Smith?

- Why do you think they meet outside Mrs Smith's house and sit on her wall?

- Why is Mrs Smith frightened of the teenagers?

Mrs Smith has moved into one of the bungalows on the edge of the grassed play area. In the spring evenings a group of teenagers regularly gather outside and sit on her garden wall. Mrs Smith feels frightened by them as they play loud music and often shout and swear at each other. Mrs Smith is too scared to go out and speak to them.

In a community people support and care for others such as very young children, disabled people and elderly people. An understanding of the needs of different people is necessary: people of different ages, races, cultures and religions, so that everyone in that community gets along with everyone else and can enjoy a peaceful community life.

Has anyone ever told you that you have a 'bad attitude'? Who told you this – a parent, a friend or a teacher? What did that person really mean – bad behaviour, being selfish, cheeky or impolite, not thinking of other people? Was the person right?

A bad attitude usually means behaviour that is unacceptable in a certain situation.

Read the comments in Figure 1.4. Sometimes people just don't stop to think about what they say or do and how it will affect others. The way people behave really does affect other people.

Being a good member of your community involves you taking responsibility for what you say and do.

I don't care.

I'll do what I like. If I want to play loud music then I will. Are you going to stop me?

I wasn't swearing – that's not bad language!

Why do people drop litter?

There's a lot of graffiti around my community!

Figure 1.4

Activities

1 Make a list of the different types of services and buildings in your community.

2 Draw in all the local facilities on a map of the area around your school.

3 a Write a list of all the local groups and organizations you can think of.

  b Tick the ones you belong to.

4 How do you help your community?

5 How has your community helped you?

6 Is your school involved with the local community?

7 Look at Figure 1.4 again. In small groups, talk about these types of attitudes and the effect they could have on other people.

Equal opportunities

What do we mean by equal opportunities?

Most people would explain this in a long sentence. What they are trying to say is that everyone should have an equal chance, and be treated fairly.

Discrimination is when a person is treated unfairly because they are different in some way.

There are many laws about equal opportunities and discrimination. Many improvements have been made over recent years.

Developing equal opportunities can begin even in nursery schools and carry on throughout the school years. In this way equality of opportunity will be expected at home, and later at work, and eventually will become part of our society.

Equal opportunities at school

Schools can encourage equal opportunities by making sure that all areas of the school are welcoming to both boys and girls and that they are both treated in exactly the same way in all lessons.

There should be no differences in the way good or bad behaviour is treated or how good work is rewarded. Teachers should not allow anyone to 'get away with' anything because of their gender. When girls and boys are treated differently, this is known as gender bias.

Displays around school, teaching materials, posters and books should all include the variety of people within society. This will show that stereotypes are misleading (a stereotype is a generally held but incorrect idea about a type of person, for example that all teenagers play loud music). It will also encourage positive attitudes and help to develop equality of opportunity for everyone whatever their gender, race, religion, culture or disability.

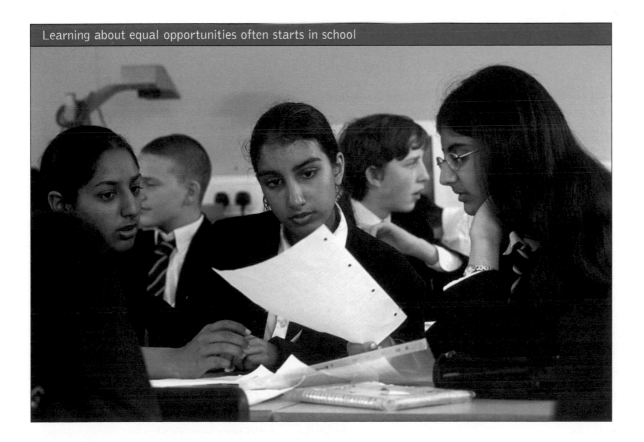

Learning about equal opportunities often starts in school

Activities that can promote equal opportunities

A number of activities could be organized in school that will help to develop equal opportunities and give a better understanding of different cultures and customs. These include:

- *a special equal opportunities day* – people from different trades and professions are asked to come into school. They talk to pupils to show how once traditional roles are changing, for example women are becoming joiners and plumbers, and men are becoming nurses and secretaries.

- *a multicultural day/evening* – people from different cultures in their traditional dress explain their customs. They might also offer samples of traditional foods.

- *inviting speakers from different religions* to talk to pupils.

- *arranging visits* to different places of worship.

A career fair at school – encouraging equal opportunities at work

The school curriculum

In school everyone should have the same opportunities in all subjects. When pupils have to make choices about which GCSEs to take, they should be encouraged to choose the subjects they are interested in and have done well in.

(A) Activities

1 Look at a copy of your school's Equal Opportunities policy and talk about it in a small group. How well do you think this policy is carried out?

2 Look at the Equal Opportunities Commission website at www.Heinemann.co.uk/hotlinks. From their home page click on 'who we are and what we do' and find out information to answer the following:

- List four issues they are campaigning about now.

- When was the EOC set up?

- The EOC deals with sex discrimination. Which organizations deal with racial and disability discrimination?

3 Look at page 23. Explain what these terms mean:

- equal opportunities
- gender bias
- stereotypes.

The Race Relations Act

The Race Relations Act 1976 set up the Commission for Racial Equality (CRE).

In 2000 changes were made to this Act. The Commission for Racial Equality has three main jobs:

- to try to prevent racial discrimination
- to encourage good relations between people from different backgrounds
- to see how the Act is really working and suggest improvements.

Your rights under the Race Relations Act

The Act makes it illegal for one person to be treated less favourably than another person because of their race, colour, nationality or cultural background.

It is illegal to print and distribute material that is likely to cause racial hatred. This would be dealt with by the police. Publishing material or adverts that could cause racial offence in the media is not allowed either.

What does all this mean?

1 Lisa is English. Her parents were born in England and her grandparents were from Jamaica. Lisa and her parents want her to go to the local comprehensive school, but she has not been given a place there.

Talk about the following questions:

- If this was because of her race, what type of discrimination would this be?
- Would it be lawful?
- Who could help Lisa's parents?

2 Uptown School has different uniform rules for boys and girls. Girls are not allowed to wear trousers and boys are not allowed to wear any head covering.

Talk about the following questions:

- Is this lawful?
- Do the uniform rules discriminate against anyone?
- What could be done about it?

(i) What is discrimination?

There are two types of racial discrimination:

1 **Direct racial discrimination** is when a person is treated less fairly than others in the same situation because of their race. For example, if a person was not offered a job because of the ethnic group they belonged to, even though they had the best qualifications and experience, this would be racial discrimination.

2 **Indirect racial discrimination** is when people from a different group are unlikely to be able to meet certain requirements, when the requirement is not based on non racial grounds. For example, if a school rule says that boys should not wear anything on their heads, this would discriminate against Asian boys who wanted to wear turbans.

What is racism?

Racism is a belief that people from a particular race or ethnic group have certain characteristics or abilities.

What is racial prejudice?

Racial prejudice is when a person forms an opinion about a race or ethnic group without real knowledge of that race or ethnic group.

A Racial Discrimination Board poster

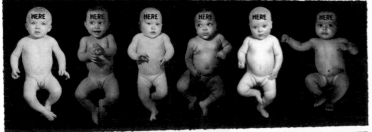

THERE ARE LOTS OF PLACES IN BRITAIN WHERE RACISM DOESN'T EXIST.

COMMISSION FOR RACIAL EQUALITY

Equal opportunities in sport

Hope for England

Three years ago Hope Powell became the first black coach to take charge of England – the women's team, that is.

You are not only the first woman and the youngest person to manage an England side, but the first black person. How did it feel when you were told?

I think I experienced every emotion. I was overwhelmed at first. It was very exciting but a bit scary too. Then I thought 'This is a once in a lifetime opportunity, I've got to do it.'

Being young, female and black I knew I could be a positive role model for young people.

I hope I can help some young black people in particular to believe in themselves and strive to be the best. I want to succeed for myself and, as the first black player in such a senior position, I want to do it for everyone else as well.

Did your family support you in your career?

My mother is West Indian and there's a very different culture there so it was a bit difficult for her to understand why a girl would want to play football. It doesn't happen in Jamaica. Now my Mum is quite proud, especially after I got this job and there was so much media coverage.

Did you experience racism in women's football when you were playing?

I remember one game when I was quite young and someone referred to me as a 'black bastard' or something. Luckily my teammate heard and she went absolutely berserk – she was five years older than me. Later when I was playing for England in Croatia this boy, he was only 12, made a Nazi salute at me. I couldn't believe it but I didn't react.

Figure 1.5 Hope Powell became manager of the England women's team in 1998, from *Kick It Out* magazine, October 2001

Education is the answer *says* Manchester United *boss Sir Alex Ferguson*

You're known as a great motivator. How do you motivate young black players to overcome racism?

All people will come up against barriers in life. The first thing you think is 'I don't deserve this.' But you have to be determined to overcome it. You've got to have a sort of blinkered approach to it, and think, 'This is not going to stop me.'

The situation today is better than it was 20 years ago, and 20 years ago it was better than 30 years ago. So progress eventually eliminates a lot of what is going on. But when the prejudice stops people getting a job, puts them out of a job, or stops them getting a place on the team because of their colour, that is real racism to me.

If you had the power to change things what would you want to change?

I think it's all down to education and how people are brought up. I was brought up in a family where there was never any prejudice. I think education from the family and school are the most important things. If parents are saying to their kids 'Don't play with that Charlie down the road because he is black,' what message does that give? I think education is the secret.

Figure 1.6 From *Kick It Out* magazine, October 2001

Children developing their skills in athletics

A Activities

1 a The Equal Opportunities Commission says that girls should have the same rights as boys to develop their sporting skills.

b The instructions to schools from the Football Association does not allow girls and boys over the age of 11 to play in the same team because football is a contact sport.

Say why you agree or disagree with these two statements. Talk about your opinions with others in your group.

2 Do you think there are equal opportunities for boys and girls in sport? Talk about this in a group.

3 Look at Figure 1.5. What types of discrimination has Hope Powell met in her career?

4 What does the interview tell you about Hope's family and culture?

5 Look at Figure 1.6. What examples of racism does Sir Alex Ferguson give?

6 Did you know that there is a national campaign to rid football of racism? Have you seen posters saying 'Give racism the red card'? Have you seen the magazine *Kick It Out* in your school?

Find out more from the *Kick It Out* website by visiting www.heinemann.co.uk/hotlinks.

Check it out

What you should have learned from this chapter

Look at the areas of study in the table. You should now know and understand the language and ideas that we have explored in Chapter 1: School.

The activities and questions in the chapter, and the worksheets your teacher will have worked through with you, should have helped you to learn about this topic.

If some of the areas are not clear, read through the pages again. If you are still not sure, ask your teacher to explain them again.

Area of study	Page
What are human rights?	9
The ECHR	9
The Human Rights Act 1998	9
The rights and responsibilities of children, parents, teachers and pupils	12–14
The different forms of power and authority	15
Who has power in school? How is this power exercised?	16
Your school community School rules and responsibilities	18
What is a community? How are you involved in your community?	21
What do we mean by equal opportunities? How schools can encourage equal opportunities	23
Equal opportunities and racism in sport	26

You should be able to answer all the following questions. These are short answer questions similar to those that will appear in Section A of the written exam paper that you will sit at the end of the course.

The knowledge and ideas covered in this chapter will also be tested in longer, more detailed questions in Sections B and D of the exam paper.

1 What does ECHR stand for?
2 How many basic human rights does the ECHR guarantee?
3 Explain what a right is.
4 Which court protects these rights?
5 List six human rights.
6 What year was the Human Rights Act passed by Parliament?
7 List four responsibilities of parents.
8 Give two rights and two responsibilities of school pupils.
9 Name an organization concerned with race relations.
10 What is the main idea behind the Children Act of 1989?
11 Explain the term 'equal opportunities'.
12 What is meant by charismatic authority?
13 What does coercion mean?
14 Who provides the funding for schools?
15 What is a community?

2 Work

Rights and responsibilities of employers and employees

Both employers and employees have legal and moral rights and responsibilities towards one another. These are explained on page 30.

A number of Acts of Parliament set out the legal responsibilities. These Acts cover different aspects of employment law.

Recruitment

Job advertisements must not be unfair to you on the grounds of race, gender or age. In other words there must be no discrimination.

The way people are chosen for the job (recruited) should make sure that the most suitable person actually gets the job.

Working in a factory

Major Acts that are concerned with employment

The Employment Rights Act 1996 is the main Act which covers employment law. According to this Act, everyone, whatever their race, gender, age or disability has equal rights and opportunities for recruitment, pay and promotion.

The Sex Discrimination Act 1975 (see page 84), **The Race Relations Act 1976** and **The Disability Discrimination Act 1995** deal with discrimination in recruitment and working practices.

The Equal Pay Act 1970, changes made in 1984, makes sure people doing the same work are paid the same.

The National Minimum Wage Act 1998 states the minimum wage that must be paid by employers to people according to their age. (For up-to-date information contact the Minimum Wage Helpline on 0845 6000 678.)

The Factories Act 1961 and **The Health and Safety Act 1974** made employers and employees responsible for health and safety at work.

The 1992 Workplace Regulations deal with EU rules, including the safe use of computers.

The EU Working Time Directive of 1998 brought in the time limit of 48 hours for a working week.

Contracts

Once you have been appointed to a job, the employer must give you (the employee) a contract.

A contract is a written document that gives the employee details about the terms and conditions of employment. The following list tells you what a contract should contain:

- name of the employer
- name of the employee
- date when the job starts
- hours of work
- rate of pay
- how and when payment will be made
- holiday entitlement
- sick pay entitlement
- pension schemes if there are any
- how to make complaints

- what the disciplinary procedures are – what happens if you do something wrong
- grievance procedures – what to do if you think the company has not treated you properly
- how to terminate (end) the employment (give in your notice).

UK money

The responsibilities of an employer	The responsibilities of an employee
To give you a contract of employment	To understand and agree the contract
To pay you the agreed wages/salary	To be punctual
To provide training in health and safety at work	To go on training courses on health and safety at work
To provide toilets and washing facilities	To follow the health and safety rules
To provide appropriate heating, lighting, and ventilation	To carry out all reasonable instructions to do with the job
To provide a safe place to work including: • safe use of equipment • safe working practices • training all workers to do their job in the correct way	To make sure they are safe and not putting anyone else at risk
To treat employees fairly	To be loyal to the company and not give away trade secrets
To allow time off work for public duties, for example going to a council meeting if elected as a councillor	
To give the right term of notice to end the employment	

Your teacher will give you more information on wages and salaries, what is meant by performance-related pay and leaving a job.

A Activities

1 Why do you think a contract is important for both the employer and employee?

2 Look at each of the responsibilities of an employer on page 30. Talk about whether these are the same as employees' rights. Write down what you all decided.

Health and safety

The HSC and HSE

Two government organizations are concerned with the health and safety of people at work.

- The Health and Safety Commission (HSC) is responsible for setting all the policies on health and safety matters.

- The Health and Safety Executive (HSE) gives advice to companies on health and safety matters. It works in partnership with local authorities to enforce the law.

The Health and Safety Executive (HSE)

The HSE makes sure that employers and employees follow the health and safety laws. It also makes sure that no harm is done to members of the public because of people's work.

The HSE makes sure the law is kept by inspecting workplaces such as building sites, factories, farms, schools and hospitals.

Local authority officers inspect shops, offices and hotels.

Health and safety inspectors have the power to order improvements to be made. They can prosecute people if the improvements are not carried out.

A Activities

1 Find out who the health and safety officer is in your school.

2 Read your school policy on health and safety. Discuss how safe your school is. Have you spotted any hazards?

3 Think about the following workplaces:
- factories
- food production lines
- offices
- building sites
- leisure centres.

What health and safety rules would you expect to find in each of these places?

Workers wearing hard hats on a building site

> **The Health and Safety Act 1974** gives employers and employees the responsibility to work together to make sure that the workplace is safe and healthy. Employers have to provide training in all parts of the job, from lifting heavy objects and using ladders to the use of electrical equipment and computers. Many companies give employees a staff handbook that contains the necessary information about their health and safety policy.
>
> It is the responsibility of employees to let their employer know if they think a situation is dangerous or unhealthy, for example smoking in offices. An employer cannot dismiss anyone for raising concerns as long as they are informed in the correct way.

The economy

What do we mean by 'the economy'?

The economy is the way in which goods, services and finances are provided and managed. Each country has its own way of organizing its national economy. There are four types of economy:

- subsistence economy – people grow their own food, gather natural resources such as fuel for their own use and build houses for themselves. They provide most of their own needs. There is little or no trade or production of goods and services, so people subsist. This type of economy is mainly found in Less Economically Developed Countries (LEDCs).

- market economy – the consumers' demand for goods and services leads the economy. Most of the businesses are privately owned. Some are multinationals. This type of economy is seen mostly in the More Economically Developed Countries (MEDCs).

- planned economy – the state owns most businesses and decides what will be produced. Consumers have little influence over the goods and services available. Most Eastern European and other former communist countries used to have this type of economy; now most have mixed economies.

- mixed economy – this is a combination of a market economy and a planned economy. Most businesses want to make a profit. They provide the goods and services people want. Some are multinationals. Other businesses are owned and run by the government. This type of economy is seen in many MEDCs.

The national economy

The UK has a mixed economy. Many businesses which produce a variety of goods and services make a profit for their owners and shareholders. Some businesses are owned and run by the state, for example the National Health Service. The utilities (the gas, electric and water companies) used to be run by the government. But during the 1980s and 1990s they were privatized so they are now run by private companies. British Rail was also privatized and different companies took over the running of various parts of the railways. There has been some discussion about nationalizing the railways again, so they would be owned and run by the government again.

The local economy

The manufacturing and service industries within an area or region of the country make up the local economy. In some parts of the country traditional types of production and manufacturing (for example ship building, steel making, coal mining) no longer exist. In these areas it is possible to obtain government grants to set up new businesses and create new jobs to bring more wealth to the people. These areas are known as Development Areas. In Development Areas, large companies can receive grants to start up in the area. This will create work for local people. In some areas grants from the EU are available.

How do businesses use financial services?

Sources of finance

Internal sources of finance are ways of raising money from inside the company. External sources of finance come mainly from banks or from selling shares (see Figure 2.1).

Figure 2.1 External and internal sources of finance

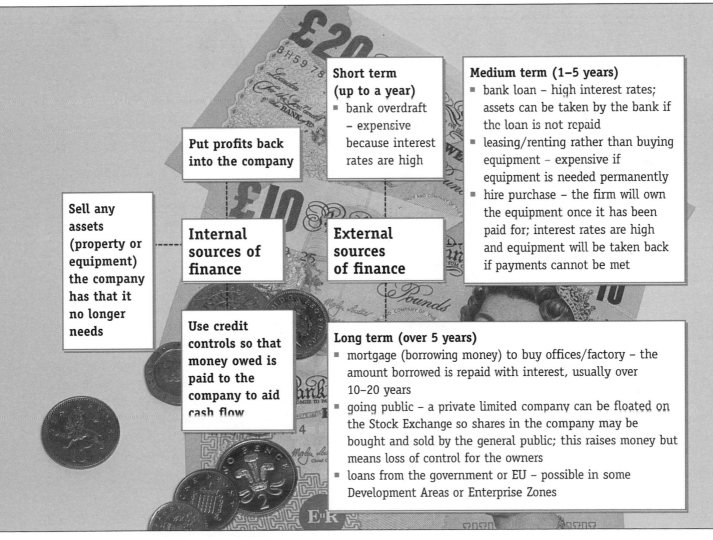

Put profits back into the company

Sell any assets (property or equipment) the company has that it no longer needs

Internal sources of finance

Use credit controls so that money owed is paid to the company to aid cash flow

External sources of finance

Short term (up to a year)
- bank overdraft – expensive because interest rates are high

Medium term (1–5 years)
- bank loan – high interest rates; assets can be taken by the bank if the loan is not repaid
- leasing/renting rather than buying equipment – expensive if equipment is needed permanently
- hire purchase – the firm will own the equipment once it has been paid for; interest rates are high and equipment will be taken back if payments cannot be met

Long term (over 5 years)
- mortgage (borrowing money) to buy offices/factory – the amount borrowed is repaid with interest, usually over 10–20 years
- going public – a private limited company can be floated on the Stock Exchange so shares in the company may be bought and sold by the general public; this raises money but means loss of control for the owners
- loans from the government or EU – possible in some Development Areas or Enterprise Zones

Banks

Banks provide business advisors to help small businesses when they are starting up.

Banks offer business bank accounts and make charges for operating these accounts. Usually a fixed charge has to be paid every time money goes in or out of the account. Phone-based banking services and some (Internet) on-line banking services are also available.

Banks will lend money to businesses as a direct loan for a fixed length of time at a rate of interest. A mortgage may be available to buy an office or factory. Some banks also offer special business insurance services.

Making deals in the city

 ### Activity

Try to organize a visit from a bank manager to talk to your group about business and personal financial matters.

Money matters – you and your money

How do ISAs work?

How old do I have to be to open a bank account?

How do people borrow money to buy a house?

What kind of account should I open when I become a student?

I have some money to save – what are the options?

How do credit cards work?

What happens if I get overdrawn?

Figure 2.2

Different types of account

To get the account to suit your needs, find out as much as you can about what different banks and building societies will offer you. Frequently, special accounts are available for young people. Most people open an ordinary current account when they start earning a living. Cash cards and credit cards are also used by many people.

To save money choose between savings accounts, investment accounts, savings bonds and ISAs (Individual Savings Accounts).

If you need to borrow money for something special such as a car, or want to take out a mortgage to buy a house – be careful. Lenders will always charge interest on the loan. Make sure you can afford to pay back the loan and the interest.

Current accounts

A current account is the most common type of account. You usually have to be eighteen or over to open a current account. Your employer will usually pay your wage or salary directly into your account. The bank will give you a cheque book and most banks offer a cash card too. You can take money out of this account by cashing a cheque or using the cash card at an ATM (Automatic Teller Machine). On-line banking is now available through the Internet.

As you know, a cash card is a small piece of plastic which contains your own personal details. You get your cash by putting the card into the cash machine and entering your PIN (Personal Identification Number) and the amount you wish to withdraw (take out). Never let anyone else use your cash card. Tell the bank if you lose it or it is stolen, as someone else could use it to get your money.

You can also arrange an overdraft on this account. This means that you make an arrangement with the bank to lend you money up to a fixed amount for a short period of time. This is then paid back to the bank. Be careful – the interest charged on the overdraft can be very high. You should never write a cheque if you know that you do not have enough money in the account to cover it. This is illegal, and is known as fraud.

Using cash cards

Savings

Savings accounts vary according to the amount you want to save. You can either save a lump sum (a fixed amount) or a regular amount each month.

Some accounts may allow you to withdraw up to a fixed amount whenever you want (without notice) without losing any interest.

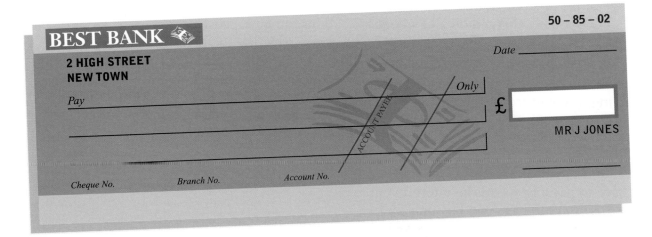

Figure 2.3 A blank cheque

Saving for that beach holiday

Other types of accounts give more interest if you agree to leave your money for a fixed term, usually a number of years – the longer the term the greater the interest.

Interest is the amount of money the account gains over a period of time given as a percentage of the amount you have in your account. Tax is usually charged on all amounts of interest.

You can also arrange to save a fixed amount each month and have that amount paid directly into a savings account from your current account.

What is an ISA?

An ISA is an Individual Savings Account. You do not have to pay any tax on the interest your money earns. You can have one ISA only and there is a limit to the amount you can save in an ISA during each tax year. It is well worth considering this type of account.

Borrowing money

Credit cards

These are issued by many financial organizations who all have the same aim – to make a profit from lending you money. The interest charged by these organizations is very high. Most cards will have an upper limit – a definite amount you can spend using the credit card.

When you use a credit card to buy goods or services the financial organization pays the bill. At the end of each month they will send you an account which gives details of what you have bought using the card, and the total amount which you owe. You now have two options – to pay the account completely and owe nothing and pay no interest, or to pay the minimum amount requested and be charged interest on the amount still to be paid. This will increase each month as you will be charged interest on the interest. Be careful – it can be very, very expensive and it is extremely easy to build up a large amount of debt in this way.

Hire purchase

This is a type of loan where you agree to pay back the amount borrowed (the cost of the item purchased, for example washing machine, TV or car) by repaying a definite amount every month. Again, interest is charged and is included within the amount to be paid back. This can be expensive – always make sure you know what the total charges are. You have three days after signing an agreement, during which you can change your mind and cancel the arrangement. Read the documents very carefully before you sign and be sure you can afford the repayments.

Companies can take back the goods if the payments are not made.

Always be very sure you understand the terms of the agreement before you sign it.

A Activities

Look at the different situations below and decide which account or method of saving would be best. Be sure you can give reasons for your answers.

- A relative wins the lottery and gives you £1000.

- You want to save for a special holiday after your exams.

- You have a Saturday job and want to save a small amount regularly.

- You are going to college and need a bank account.

Types of business

In the UK different types of business operate in different sectors of the mixed economy.

A sole trader is a business owned and run by one person – the owner. The owner will probably employ other people, but the owner controls everything, takes all the risks and keeps all the profits. If the business is unsuccessful, the owner would be entirely responsible for any debts. There are 3–4 million sole traders in this country.

A partnership is an agreement between two or more people to set up and run a company. The partners provide the finance, make decisions and share all the risks and responsibilities of running the business.

A public limited company (plc) must have a board of directors who run the company, and must hold annual general meetings for its shareholders. A shareholder is someone who

Market day – a traditional way of doing business

has bought shares in a company and so owns part of the company. The shares are traded on the Stock Exchange and may be bought by individuals or organizations.

A private limited company (Ltd) is usually made up of a small number of people (at least two) who buy shares in the company and so become part owners of the company. The shares are not traded on the Stock Exchange and can only be bought by the people who started the company.

In a **co-operative** all the workers buy shares in the business and it is therefore owned by all the workers. Everyone is involved in the finance and decision-making of the company.

Industry sectors

All businesses are in trade to make a profit. They provide services or manufacture products. All production is divided into one of the following sectors.

- **The primary sector** takes raw materials and natural resources from the ground or sea by mining, quarrying or fishing. It also includes farming. Animals are classed as a natural resource for these purposes, so farmers who breed animals for slaughter are included in this sector.

- **The secondary sector** uses the raw materials and natural resources gathered or grown by the primary sector and makes (manufactures) them into a completed product, for example frozen pizza, cars, houses.

- **The tertiary sector** is the service sector. A service may be provided to industry, such as advertising or distribution of goods, or to consumers such as shops and supermarkets, pubs or leisure centres. Services such as education, the police, fire service and the National Health Service are also included in this sector.

- **The quaternary sector** is also a service sector. This is a specialized sector which has developed as a result of the technological advances made during the last few years. This sector involves telecommunications and the Internet. It includes services such as call centres and on-line banking and shopping.

(A) Activity

Write four headings:

- Primary sector
- Secondary sector
- Tertiary sector
- Quaternary sector.

Under each heading for each sector give as many examples as you can.

A busy call centre

Case study: Nissan Motor Manufacturing (UK) Ltd

The company

Japan is the home of Nissan, a multinational car manufacturing company. In 1984 Nissan chose an airfield in Sunderland in the north-east of England as the site for setting up its centre of production for passenger cars in Europe. This brought much-needed investment into the region as the traditional ship-building, steel-production and coal-mining industries were in decline.

The site was chosen because:

- it was a large area (300 hectares) of flat land that could easily be built on
- there were very good road and rail links to all parts of the country and two sea ports were nearby
- the local people and trade unions had positive attitudes
- the area had an excellent name for engineering
- the site was in an Enterprise Zone and a grant of £100 million was available.

The company has spent over £1.5 billion on the car plant. The production of cars began in 1986. Between 1986 and 2002 more than 2 million cars were made in Sunderland. Of these, 1.4 million were exported to 58 different countries.

Nissan has created 5000 jobs within the car plant itself. Another 10 000 jobs have been created within the area by other companies making parts for the car plant.

The employees

People applying for a job at Nissan have to complete a range of tests, practical exercises and interviews successfully. In 1999, 800 new staff were appointed out of 11 000 applicants.

While the site was being developed in 1985 Nissan negotiated a single union deal with the AEU (Amalgamated Engineering Union). There have not been any industrial disputes. As part of the agreement with the AEU a company council was set up. Employees are elected to serve as members of council for a term of four years. This has been very successful in keeping good relationships between the company, the employees and the union.

Nissan operates a 'Single Policy Status'. This means that all employees have equal opportunity, the same terms and conditions of employment, and enjoy the same company benefits. The work of employees is monitored and employees are informed about their performance. Targets are set and reviewed every year.

Health and safety

The health and safety section within the company deals with safety (from the design stage onwards), occupational health, hygiene,

The Nissan factory in Sunderland

fire prevention, and health and safety training. Health and safety are essential and everyone has their part to play. All new employees go through health and safety training as part of their introduction to the company. In the design of the car assembly line and the manufacturing equipment, health and safety are very important.

Car production

The production of cars at Nissan works around the JIT (Just In Time) principle. This means 'using the minimum amount of resources in the most efficient way'. Small batches of parts are delivered frequently so that the Nissan plant does not have to store, move or check the quality of the parts. This means costs are cut.

Fewer people are needed to move and handle car parts and the quality controls are operated by the supplier, again cutting labour costs.

Employees work in teams with a supervisor who will check the quality and speed of their work. Each employee is able to cover three jobs within an area, so each job can be done by three people, allowing flexibility.

Robots

Over 250 robots are used on the production line. Most robots are used in the body shop for jobs such as spot welding and sealing inner and outer panels. Robots are also used in the paint shop to apply undercoat and sealers and in the final assembly shop to seal lights and windscreens.

Robots are used because they can

- work in areas that are unsuitable for people
- remove the boredom of jobs that have to be done over and over again
- produce a finish that is always of the same quality.

Environmentally friendly?

With any large-scale manufacturing plant pollution is a danger to the environment. Nissan take great care to do as much as possible for the local environment. Noise from the press plant is cut to the minimum and the plant is said to be one of the quietest in Europe.

The suppliers use packaging which can be returned to them after use. Parts are collected from each supplier and delivered all together rather than being delivered separately from all

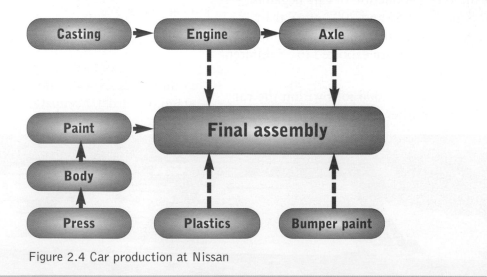

Figure 2.4 Car production at Nissan

over Europe. This is thought to cut the transport distance by about 100 million kilometres and to save 32 million litres of fuel.

Forty hectares of the original site have been kept as environmental areas for wildlife. There is a reservoir for wildfowl and a wildflower meadow has been created to encourage wildlife.

The local economy

The opening of the Nissan Motor Manufacturing plant in Sunderland has done much to help the local and regional economy and increase prosperity for the north-east of England.

Many companies within the region now supply parts to Nissan. Over 200 companies from around the UK and Europe supply goods worth more than £1 billion to the Nissan plant each year. Some of the suppliers have moved their businesses near to the Nissan plant. Nissan believe that 'Sunderland is now the UK's fastest growing automotive manufacturing centre'.

It has been estimated that Nissan contributes around £400 million every year to the local economy. This is a much-needed boost to the local and regional economy, as many traditional manufacturing companies have closed.

Nissan Motor Manufacturing (UK) has developed partnerships with schools – 2500 pupils visit the plant every year. The company has sponsored well-known sporting events such as a series of The Great North Run and the Yellow Brick Road Rally to raise funds for a hospice.

Putting the final touches to Nissan cars, Sunderland

Nissan cars being put together on the factory floor

The national economy

In the 1980s the government gave grants of money to companies which set up businesses in Enterprise Zones. A grant of £100 million was given to Nissan. However, since then Nissan has spent over £1.5 billion on the Sunderland car plant. The company has created over 15 000 permanent jobs (in a region where unemployment is still high) and put millions of pounds into the local and therefore national economy.

(A) Activities

1   Look back to the section on industry sectors on page 38. What type of production is carried out at Nissan – primary, secondary, tertiary or quaternary? Explain your answer.

2   Look at page 39. Explain what Nissan's Single Policy Status means.

3   Look at pages 39–40. What does the health and safety section within the company deal with?

4   How many jobs have been created in the area? Why are these jobs important to the region?

5   Look at pages 40–41. List three ways in which the Nissan car plant is environmentally friendly.

What's your opinion of work experience?

It's just working for nothing.

Work experience is a week off school.

?

I'm looking forward to doing something different for a change.

It's a great opportunity.

Figure 2.5 Opinions of work experience

Learning new skills on work experience

The success of your work experience placement really does depend on your approach to it. If you are interested, show that you are willing to learn, are polite and ask sensible questions, you will gain a great deal. Use the time wisely: discover more about the company and the people – then you will probably enjoy it *and* give a good impression of your school.

If you are presenting work experience as your coursework for the examination, you must make sure that you include evidence for all the sections of the mark scheme.

Your teacher will guide you through this and there is more help in Section 4, which is all about coursework and the exam.

A Activities

Produce a case study of a company of your choice.

1 **Find out about:**

- the type of company (partnership, limited company, etc.)
- how the company is organized
- how people are chosen for jobs
- equal opportunities
- health and safety policy
- links with other businesses
- contribution to the economy.

2 **Use your ICT skills and try to include:**

- a graph or chart
- a photograph or picture of the company
- a picture or drawing of the product the company makes, if it is a manufacturing business
- a map to show where the business is.

Check it out

What you should have learned from this section

Look at the areas of study in the table. You should now know and understand the language and ideas that we have explored in Chapter 2: Work.

The activities and questions in the chapter, and the extra sheets your teacher will have worked through with you, should have helped you to learn about this topic.

If some of the areas are not clear, read through the pages again. If you are still not sure, ask your teacher to explain them again.

Area of study	Page
The laws affecting employment	29
The rights and responsibilities of employers and employees	29–30
Contracts of employment	30
Health and safety at work	31
The economy and business finance	32–34
Your money	34–36
Business and industry – types of business and industry sectors	37–38

You should be able to answer all the following questions. These are short answer questions similar to those that will appear in Section A of the written exam paper that you will sit at the end of the course.

The knowledge and ideas covered in this chapter will also be tested in longer, more detailed questions in Sections B and D of the exam paper.

1. Name three Acts of Parliament which are concerned with employment.
2. What is a contract of employment?
3. List three responsibilities of an employer.
4. What does HSC stand for?
5. What does the Health and Safety Executive do?
6. What is a credit card?
7. What does plc stand for? Give an example.
8. List three different types of production and give examples of each one.
9. Explain the term 'a mixed economy'.
10. Name two ways a company could raise extra finance.
11. Why is the Health and Safety Act 1974 important?

3 Local community

Community life

We are going to look at three specific areas that can make up community life – ethnic identity, religion and culture.

Stereotypes

A stereotype is when we have a *fixed* idea of who, or what, someone or something is. People often stereotype ethnic groups, a religion, or a culture. These fixed ideas can affect community life.

Ethnic identity

The term ethnic identity or ethnicity is often used to refer to minority (small) groups within a society. Ethnic identity refers to a particular way of life, the language, lifestyle and customs of a group within a community.

When people of different ethnic identities live in a community the culture of that community is much more varied. Sometimes this can cause problems if one ethnic group feels it is being treated unfairly. When this happens it is usually headline news, as reported in 2001 in cities such as Bradford (your teacher may give you a sheet about this topic).

Ethnic identity takes many forms …

Religion

Religion is a general term which means a belief in a particular faith, set of values, practices and worship – often of an invisible supernatural power or being.

Members of a particular religion will be expected to conform to certain beliefs and practices. This will affect their attitudes and behaviour.

- Followers of a religion will often meet together to worship. They have a belief in that religion, share a set of values, and help and support each other.

- The religion will set out very clear rules of behaviour and what will happen if this code of behaviour is not followed. This has a powerful effect in controlling behaviour throughout a person's life.

A local place of worship can be a meeting place as well as a place of spiritual worship. A number of social activities may be organized by members of the religious community which benefit the whole community, for example a toddler group or playgroup for pre-school children, after-school clubs, a youth club.

Many people in the community will use these facilities without being members of the religious community.

Religion can sometimes cause trouble in a community if followers of different religions do not tolerate each other's beliefs. This can result in tension and conflict which may lead to violence. This would disturb normal peaceful community life.

(A) Activities

1 How many different religions can you think of?

2 Make a list or an ideas web of all the different religions your group can think of.

3 Talk about which different religions are practised in your community.

4 Can you think of any conflicts that have been caused by religion?

Who worships here?

Culture

The term 'culture' means the shared language, behaviours, customs, traditions and values of a society. The values in society refer to things that people believe are important and worthwhile. Values will change over time even within the same society or group, but these changes do not happen quickly. The values different ethnic groups have will vary too.

Children learn their culture by a process known as socialisation.

Ethnic groups will have their own particular traditions, customs and values. These may be similar to, or very different from, the culture of most people in the community.

Community life can be enriched for all people within a community if everyone is willing to accept each other's culture and live peacefully as neighbours.

Notting Hill Carnival

Community life can be affected by clashes of different cultures when people are unwilling to understand others. This can lead to tension or disturbances which interrupt peaceful community life.

(A) Activities

1 Find information about a different culture from your own. You could find out about cultures – your own culture and one other of your choice. How would you describe the following with regard to each culture?

- type of family
- marriage
- how children are brought up
- how children are educated
- fashions and dress code
- popular music
- food, diet and eating patterns
- religion
- festivals celebrated.

2 Different groups within the same society, for example teenagers, may have slightly different behaviour and values from the wider culture they belong to. In a small group, talk about the ways in which a teenage culture is different.

Local government

Local government systems

There are normally two levels of local government:

- Town, city, district and county councils and unitary authorities meet in town or city halls, district council offices, civic centres or shire halls. Councillors serve a term of four years. They are responsible for council housing, education, police and fire services, paving and street lighting, roads, libraries, arts, leisure and sports, and social services. Councils receive money from the council tax and from taxes raised by the national government.

Local councillors in council chambers

- Parish councils are elected within a parish area. Parish councillors are elected to serve a maximum of four years. They are responsible for local services: village halls, playing fields and rights of way. Their money comes from a small part of the council tax.

A new constitution for local authorities

In 2000 the government told all local authorities in the country that they must set up a new constitution. They had to choose between:

- a leader with a cabinet of councillors (see Figure 3.1)

- a directly elected mayor with a cabinet of councillors

- a directly elected mayor with a council manager.

Local authorities asked people, organizations and businesses about their preferred choice for their area. Some local authorities arranged a referendum. This means that people on the register of electors for the area could vote for their choice of constitution. The register of electors is a list of the names and addresses of all people who have the right to vote. All local

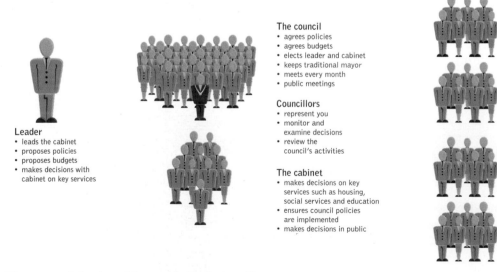

Leader
- leads the cabinet
- proposes policies
- proposes budgets
- makes decisions with cabinet on key services

The council
- agrees policies
- agrees budgets
- elects leader and cabinet
- keeps traditional mayor
- meets every month
- public meetings

Councillors
- represent you
- monitor and examine decisions
- review the council's activities

The cabinet
- makes decisions on key services such as housing, social services and education
- ensures council policies are implemented
- makes decisions in public

Overview and scrutiny committees
- non-executive
- wide legal powers to look into cabinet matters
- cabinet and officers must attend
- public meeting

Development control panel
- decides planning applications
- enforces planning control/building regulations
- public meetings

Licensing panel
- licences – taxis and taxi drivers
- public entertainment
- street collections/lotteries
- sports ground safety certificates
- registering marriage premises
- public meetings

Standards committee
- maintains standards of council conduct
- advises on specific ethical issues
- independent chair
- public meetings

Figure 3.1 A leader with a cabinet of councillors
This is based on the proposed system at Gateshead Council

authorities have to make sure that their decisions are closely monitored.

Financing local services

A local council raises money through the council tax. It also receives money from central government for development and specific projects, for example meeting the costs of national pay awards.

The local council spends money according to the council policy on:

- education
- social services
- leisure
- housing
- libraries
- cleansing
- community events
- repairs
- roads
- lighting
- parks
- environmental issues.

The amount of money the council chooses to spend on each of these areas affects the quality of people's lives on a daily basis.

It is very important to vote in all elections. It is your opportunity to choose who you want to represent you.

If you feel that the council is not taking your needs into account you can arrange to meet your local councillor, or go to a surgery which your local councillors hold regularly, and express your views.

Council workers

 Activities

1 Find out what system of government your area has at local level. How was the decision to choose this option made?

2 Find out where your local council meets.

3 What are the names of your local councillors? Which political party, if any, do they represent?

4 Find out the names of the leader of your local council and the person responsible for education on the council.

5 Try to attend a council meeting to find out how decisions about your area are made.

6 Name the departments in your local council.

Devolution – regional government in the UK

Devolution is the transfer of power to a lower level, especially from central government to local or national administrators. For centuries, Britain has had a central government. Now there is a Scottish Parliament and Assemblies in Northern Ireland and Wales (Figure 3.2). Some people think that there should be an English Parliament to look after the issues relating to England. Other people believe that a central government does not understand the needs of regions within England, so there should be regional assemblies.

A Activities

1 Find the names and political parties of the first ministers of Scotland, Northern Ireland and Wales using the Internet.

2 Look at Figure 3.2.
   a Which Parliament or Assembly has the power to raise taxes for its country?
   b List two things that all three have the power to make decisions about.

	Scottish Parliament	Welsh Assembly	Northern Ireland Assembly
Meets in	Edinburgh	Cardiff	Belfast
Number of members	129	60	108
Method of election	Additional member system	Additional member system	Single transferable vote
Powers	• Can increase taxes for Scotland beyond national tax level and use money in Scotland • Makes decisions about issues relating to regional affairs, education and health spending • Makes new laws for Scotland – as a result is responsible for home affairs in Scotland	• Cannot raise taxes • Cannot make separate laws for Wales • Makes decisions about regional affairs, education, health authorities, local government	• Makes decisions about education, health and local government • Takes the lead in economic development • Required by Good Friday Agreement of 1998 to take part in talks with Irish Republic about common issues such as transport and agriculture

Figure 3.2

Voting systems

The 'first past the post' system is used in the UK to elect national government. Many people argue that this system is not truly representative of the way people vote in elections. For example, in the 1997 general election the Labour Party took 63 per cent of the seats in Parliament with 43 per cent of the votes. The Conservative Party in Wales and Scotland won no seats, although they had 20 per cent of votes in Wales and 18 per cent of votes in Scotland. The Electoral Reform Society and other pressure groups would argue that Labour voters are over-represented and Conservative voters are under-represented in Parliament through the 'first past the post' system. They think that the voting system should be changed.

After the 1997 general election the government set up a commission, headed by Lord Jenkins, to look at how the voting system could be changed. The Jenkins Commission examined different voting systems, particularly proportional systems that keep a link between MPs and the people in their constituencies. In these systems the number of seats in Parliament a party wins is directly related to the overall percentage of votes the party receives.

The Jenkins Commission Report, published in October 1998, recommended that a system called AV plus should be introduced. This is the Alternative Vote System with a top-up element. The top-up element means 15–20 per cent of MPs would be chosen by cities, districts or counties. A referendum is proposed to ask people if they would like to change to the new system.

Activities

1 What system was used in the 1997 general election?

2 Which do you think is the fairest system – the 'first past the post' system or the Alternative Vote System? Give reasons for your choice.

Voting systems

'First past the post' system
- Every voter has one vote.
- The candidate with the most votes in each constituency wins a seat in Parliament.
- Even though the party with the second highest number of votes might have been close behind the winner, those votes do not count towards the number of seats the second party wins in Parliament.

Alternative Vote System
- Each constituency elects one MP.
- Voters place numbers against the names of candidates in their order of choice.
- All the first choice candidates are counted. A candidate must have more than 50 per cent of the votes to win.
- If no candidate receives 50 per cent, the candidate with the smallest number of votes is removed from the list.
- The voters' second choice candidates are counted and added to the first choice candidates' totals.

- This continues until only one candidate remains.

Single transferable vote – used to elect members of local, regional and European government in Northern Ireland
- There are fewer constituencies and each constituency has a larger number of MPs.
- Voters place numbers against the names of candidates in their order of choice.
- The number of votes a candidate needs to win the seat is worked out according to the total number of electors.
- If the winning candidate gets more than this number of votes, the extra votes are given to other candidates.

Additional member system – used for elections to the Scottish Parliament and the Welsh Assembly
- Half the members are elected using the 'first past the post' system.
- The other half are chosen according to the percentage of votes won by each party.

How individuals can bring about change

Political parties

A political party is a collection of individuals who meet at local, regional and national level with other individuals who share the same political views. They form national parties to try to win power at election time by pooling resources and ideas.

At election time each political party produces a manifesto. This sets out the type of action the party will take if it is elected to form the government at local or national level.

The three main political parties in Britain are the Conservative Party, the Labour Party and the Liberal Democrats. In Wales and Scotland there are active national parties. These are the Scottish Nationalist Party and Plaid Cymru. In Northern Ireland the political parties are split into three camps – the Unionist parties, the Social Democratic Labour Party and Sinn Fein.

The Green Party campaigning

Smaller parties include the Green Party, the National Front, the Socialist Party and the UK Independence Party. These smaller parties tend to concentrate on specific issues.

Political parties produce policies at meetings and conferences. They hope to win power at elections so they can make changes in the country.

Voluntary organizations

Voluntary organizations are groups of people who:

- inform the general public about conditions some people live in

- raise money to help make the situation better

- create activities and opportunities for members of the local community to meet and share common experiences

- create opportunities for young people

- undertake work in the community to support others.

Many voluntary organizations are charities. The work of raising and collecting money is done by locally organized groups of individuals who work voluntarily.

National organizations such as Childline raise awareness in the general public about the problems facing children. People then choose to support the work of the organization by donating money and time to its activities. Childline becomes a voice for children and its views are considered at national level.

A 'Fun run' for charity

At international level the work of charities, such as Oxfam, Save the Children and the Red Cross, is very important in the management of disasters. Charities also help countries in other ways, for example by working with them to develop healthcare, education and safe drinking water systems.

Charities work to inform the public and change attitudes and conditions. For example in early 2002 the Red Cross were active in trying to make sure the first prisoners from Afghanistan were recognized as prisoners of war so they would be given fair treatment.

Voluntary organizations work in the local community. They include youth clubs and sports groups. A list of the voluntary organizations in your area is available from your local council.

Pressure groups

A pressure group is a collection of people who aim to influence or change government policy. Pressure groups usually focus on one issue or area of government policy, which will affect people at local as well as national level. They are well organized and explain their ideas to the general public to gain support. They will have a group headquarters, membership with fees and, probably, a web page. There are a wide range of pressure groups in Britain including:

- those representing employers, for example the Confederation of British Industry

- those representing employees, for example trade unions and professional associations

- those supporting a cause or issue, for example the Campaign for Nuclear Disarmament

- those wishing to influence an area of government policy, for example the Countryside Alliance

- those challenging international injustices, for example Amnesty International.

Some organizations work on an international scale and relate to national and European government and the United Nations. These

Amnesty International is campaigning against the use of child soldiers in Uganda

organizations include Greenpeace, Amnesty International and the Red Cross. Some pressure groups are very successful because people agree with their cause and join the organization. This may be why some pressure groups have a growing membership while membership of political parties is falling.

Supporters of pressure groups have argued that they are more effective than political parties. Pressure groups try to influence events and decision-making in their area of interest. These areas might be the environment, human rights, the countryside, employment law, education, discrimination, health and disability rights.

Focus groups

A focus group is a collection of individuals, often with different backgrounds and political beliefs, who join together because of a common focus. A group will usually focus on issues that relate to the local community, such as closing a school or plans for a new road. Focus groups meet until the problem they are facing has been solved. They often take advice from national organizations and some have been known to challenge decisions in court.

A focus group protests against cuts in education

(A) Activities

1 Visit www.heinemann.co.uk/hotlinks and find out the main aims of the three pressure groups: Greenpeace, Amnesty International and the Red Cross. Which one would you join and why?

2 If you joined a political party, which one would it be and why?

3 Contact your local council and ask for the list of voluntary organizations in your area. Vote for the organization you are most interested in and arrange for a representative to come and talk to your group about its work.

4 Find out if there are any focus groups in your community. What problem are they focusing on?

Formal consultation

When the government wants to build a new road or start a new building project, then local councils are informed. The plans are made available to members of the public and public meetings are held. The public's views and opinions are heard at these meetings, though it is also possible to put your opinion about a plan in writing. Strong public opposition from individuals to a proposal can lead to plans being changed or dropped.

If the government feels it is necessary, it will call a public inquiry into a problem. These are very formal proceedings. Members of the public usually organize themselves into a focus group and arrange to be represented at the inquiry. The inquiry chairperson will then produce a report and present it to the government for consideration.

Trade unions

One example of a pressure group is a trade union. This is a group of workers who all do the same kind of job or trade. The union will look after the common interests of its members.

Membership of a union does not depend on age, race, gender, political or religious belief, or social status. However, the Trades Union Congress (TUC), which is an organization of trade unions, has been linked with the Labour movement and the Labour Party throughout its history.

This has given the TUC an influence on the policy-making of British governments. As a group, trade unions have one power that is unavailable to other pressure groups – the power of striking or working to rule. Striking means that a worker stops working until the union demands are met. Working to rule means that workers refuse to do any work that is not set out in their contract until the disagreement has been settled.

Trade unions supporting Post Office workers in recent strikes

Trade unions hold routine meetings with employers to promote health and safety issues, to discuss pay and conditions of service and to develop the industry to everyone's benefit. They also represent workers in court cases which may end in improved working conditions for individuals. This legal work has acted as a trigger for other reforms and legislation.

Lobbyists

MPs meet people who come to talk to them in the central lobby (large hall) of the Houses of Parliament. The term 'lobbyist' comes from this. Lobbyists meet individuals or groups of MPs and persuade them to take up their cause. This means asking questions in the House of Commons and raising issues at committee meetings.

A lobbyist is usually a professional person who is employed to try to influence or change government decisions. Lobbyists are employed by a range of groups including trade unions, companies, pressure groups and charities. Lobbyists help their clients by:

- telling them who is the most appropriate person to approach
- arranging meetings between MPs, ministers and clients
- suggesting ways to influence decisions
- preparing a timetable for the lobby and arranging media coverage.

Protests

The now historical Campaign for Nuclear Disarmament (CND), marching in 1958

Peaceful protest is legal in Britain. There have been many protests throughout British history which have brought issues to the attention of the public. These protests usually take the form of marches with banners and placards. An alternative method is to deliver a petition to government. Major protests have drawn attention to issues such as votes for women, unemployment, nuclear disarmament, pensions, war, fuel costs and disability rights. The government usually takes the views of peaceful protesters into account when debating in Parliament or considering changes to policy.

Keeping pressure lawful

Pressure groups must choose the way they try to influence public and government opinion carefully. Sometimes they will carry out a public opinion survey to test public opinion and strength of feeling towards an issue. Sometimes they will use the media to argue their point of view, or place an advertisement. Sometimes they will promote a specific cause on a particular day or week, for example National No Smoking Day is usually one Wednesday in March.

Unlawful pressure is applied when a person causes civil disobedience by breaking the law using non-violent means. For example the environmentalist, Swampy, broke the law in a dispute about a second runway at Manchester Airport by occupying land without permission. Very few pressure groups use violent protest, though the Animal Liberation Group has attacked property where experiments take place.

Environmentalists, protesting to save our trees

Activities

A

1 What does a trade union do?

2 Find out if your local council is consulting the public over any plans at present and try to attend a meeting.

3 List three issues which you consider should be the subject for a protest. Explain why you have chosen these three.

Case study: Making changes

For a number of years people who worked part time or had fixed-term contracts did not have the same rights and entitlements as full-time workers. This led to many disputes and much inequality.

People who had full-time jobs had many more days holiday. Bank holidays were extra days holiday in some companies, but not in others. There was great variation and no minimum number of days holiday. Something had to be done so that part-time workers or people on short-term or fixed-term contracts were treated equally.

All the trade unions campaigned for equality for all workers. It is only within the last four years that this has been brought about. This has been done in two main ways:

- The Working Time Regulations 1998 limited the length of the working day and week. It gave all workers the right to at least four weeks' paid holiday after thirteen weeks of employment.

- The Part Time Workers' Regulations 2000 gave all part-time workers the same entitlements as full-time workers.

The great holiday hijack

Some bosses are still opposing paid holidays three years after the law changed, says Neasa MacErlean.

If someone asked you to name the biggest cause of disputes over employment rights, you might say the minimum wage, long hours, maternity benefit or pensions. Yet employment advisers dealing with the public agree that holidays cause most hassles.

'It's easily the biggest single employment issue that Citizens Advice Bureaux deal with right across the country,' says Richard Dunstan of the National Association of Citizens Advice Bureaux (Nacab), which together deal with 600,000 employment queries a year. Richard says that many people at the low-paid end of the workforce are losing out. 'Many people aren't getting paid holiday at all, or less than the four weeks. This issue tends to go along with long hours and poor conditions.'

The Low Pay Unit says a third of the calls it receives are to do with time off.

'It generates an enormous number of phone calls,' says Sarah Veale of the TUC, which gives out free leaflets on employment issues to callers to its free information line.

At Acas, The Advisory Conciliation and Arbitration Service, too, there is continuing demand for advice.

Figure 3.3 Adapted from an article in the *Observer*, 24 February 2002.

A Activities

1 Why was it necessary to make changes to holiday entitlements?

2 Who campaigned for change?

3 Find out more about one trade union. How has it acted as a pressure group to bring about a change which has benefited its members?

4 What is The Low Pay Unit? What does it do? You could look on their website at www.heinemann.co.uk/hotlinks to find out more.

Check it out

What you should have learned from this chapter

Look at the areas of study in the table. You should now know and understand the language and ideas that we have explored in Chapter 3: Local community.

The activities and questions in the chapter, and the extra sheets your teacher will have worked through with you, should have helped you to learn about this topic.

If some of the areas are not clear, read through the pages again. If you are still not sure, ask your teacher to explain them again.

Area of study	Page
How ethnic identity, religion and culture can affect community life	45–47
How local councils work	48–49
Regional government and devolution	50
The Scottish Parliament	50
The Welsh Assembly	50
The Northern Ireland Assembly	50
Political parties	52
Voluntary organizations	52
Pressure groups	53
Trade unions	55

You should be able to answer all the following questions. These are short answer questions similar to those that will appear in Section A of the written exam paper that you will sit at the end of the course.

The knowledge and ideas covered in this chapter will also be tested in longer, more detailed questions in Sections B and D of the exam paper.

1 Explain what you understand by the terms:
   • ethnic identity
   • religion
   • culture.
2 Describe the three ways a local council could be organized.
3 What is devolution?
4 Name the three devolved powers and say where they are based.
5 What voting system do we use to elect Members of Parliament?
6 Name three pressure groups.
7 Choose one pressure group and give an example of how it has influenced an issue.
8 What does TUC stand for?
9 List four political parties.
10 Name a voluntary organization and say what it does.

National and European citizenship

Key ideas

What about the Chinese government-directed massacre at Tiananmen Square? Who were the criminals here – the protesters or the government?

What is crime? Most people agree that the murder of Stephen Lawrence was a racially motivated crime (these are the five suspects after they had been found not guilty). Can a person who has not been charged for an offence ever be brought to trial again for the same crime?

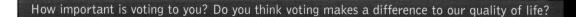

How important is voting to you? Do you think voting makes a difference to our quality of life?

Do you believe everything you read, see and hear in the media?

4 National and European government

Systems of government

Different systems of government are in place across the world.

The Queen at the State opening of parliament

ⓘ Systems of government

A **republic** is lead by a government. There is no monarch.

A **one-party state** has only one political party.

A **constitutional monarchy** has an elected government and a monarch (a king or queen) as head of state.

A **dictatorship** is ruled by one person who has the power to say what happens in all matters.

The system of government in the UK

The United Kingdom is a democracy. This means that it has a free and fair voting system, freedom of speech and a choice of political parties at elections.

The United Kingdom is a constitutional monarchy. The Queen is the head of state but Parliament has the power of government.

Ⓐ Activities

1 If you were asked to set up a school council, which system of government would you choose? Explain your choice.

2 Look on the European Union website.

a Find three EU countries which are republics.

b Name three constitutional monarchies.

The democratic system in the UK

A democracy is built up over time. Through a country's constitution a democracy hopes to encourage people to debate issues and take part in the democratic process.

Coming of age in the UK democracy

The electoral process in the UK allows people over the age of eighteen, whose names appear on the register of electors, to vote in elections to choose their representatives at local, national and European level. Sometimes the candidates are not members of political parties, and are therefore 'independent'. Mostly, candidates are connected to a political party. The finance for election campaigns comes from the party's membership fees and donations from supporters.

Elections

An election is called and nominations for candidates for the election are invited by the closing date. Candidates start on a campaign for election. This will involve canvassing for

(i)

Political party – an organized group of people with similar views and beliefs, who have a written constitution and manifesto on which they fight an election.

Candidate – someone who has been chosen to run for election as a representative of a political party. Candidates must be over the age of 21.

Election campaign – the set of activities, such as party political broadcasts, which are designed to gain your vote.

Polling station – a building which on election day is a place where you can go to vote, for example your local school.

MP – Member of Parliament. The candidate who has been elected for an area.

Surgery – in this case, where people can go to talk to their MP about problem issues in their area, for example housing.

Cabinet – group of senior ministers in the government who are responsible for specific areas, such as health or education. The Cabinet decides government policy.

A polling station on election day

votes (trying to persuade people to vote for them) and producing election leaflets. In national elections, party political broadcasts are used to explain ideas.

Voting takes place on a stated day at a local polling station. The votes are taken in sealed boxes to a central counting place. After counting, the returning officer for the area makes a public declaration of the results.

Parliament

Each MP is elected to serve an area of the country called a constituency for a maximum of five years. During that time, they debate issues at the Houses of Parliament at Westminster in London. They are responsible for deciding:

- taxes to fund public services
- laws, rules and regulations relating to areas such as:
  - education
  - health
  - defence issues
  - law and order
  - international relations
  - home affairs.

MPs also hold regular surgeries in their constituencies where people can come to talk to them about any issues that concen them.

What happens next?

After an election, the party which has won the largest number of seats becomes the ruling party for the council or government for the next five years.

At local level: the council leader arranges for council members to vote for a group of councillors who will make the important decisions.

At national level: the Prime Minister appoints a group of MPs to be ministers and help run the country. A group of senior ministers and secretaries of state form the Cabinet. The rest of the MPs who do not hold government office are known as backbenchers.

The political party that won the second largest number of seats at the election becomes the official Opposition. The Leader of the Opposition will ask members of their political party to act as Opposition spokespeople on aspects of government such as health or education. This group of people become the Shadow Cabinet. All MPs who do not belong to the political party in power are opposition MPs.

A Activities

1 Find out the following about your school's local MP:

- name
- party the MP represents
- main beliefs
- role in government.

2 Who is the Leader of the Opposition?

Conservative, Michael Portillo, losing his constituency (1997)

How national government works

The main political parties in Parliament

The Labour Party	The Conservative Party	The Liberal Democrat Party
Labour www.labour.org.uk (formed in the early 20th century)	**Conservatives** (formed in the 18th century)	**LIBERAL DEMOCRATS** (formed in 1988)
Education → • believes the state and private companies should work together and that more funding should be given to education	• believes in a greater role for private companies – private money should be added to public spending	• wants to increase income tax by 1p in the pound to spend on education
Health → • believes in more funding for the NHS and cutting waiting lists	• believes in a free market between doctors' surgeries and hospitals as a way to improve performance	• wants to cut waiting lists; believes in free dental and eye tests
Europe → • believes in joining the single currency when the time is right for Britain	• is against the single currency, though some of the party are pro-European and there has been disagreement	• believes that Britain should join the single currency as soon as possible

Figure 4.1 The main political parties in Parliament and their policies

Activities

1 Which of the parties would you support from the brief outline of their policies given above? Why?

2 What are your beliefs about education, health and Europe? Discuss in groups.

3 Choose another issue important to the UK, such as transport. Look at the Labour party website on www.heinemann.co.uk/hotlinks and find out more. What would you do differently?

The House of Commons

MPs sit in the House of Commons. The main function of the House of Commons is to make the laws by which the country is governed and managed.

Debating in the House of Commons

An issue is debated by putting a motion in Parliament. At the end of each debate the Speaker (the MPs' chairperson) will ask those MPs in favour of the motion to say 'aye' and those against to say 'no'. If the Speaker cannot tell which side has won, the division bell is rung. This tells MPs that the Speaker is calling a division. A division means that the MPs must go to one of two rooms on each side of the House of Commons. The 'ayes' go one way and the 'nos' go the other. Forty MPs must vote before a decision can be made. Two MPs from each side of the debate count the votes. The Speaker then announces the results.

Committees

A large amount of the work in Parliament is done by select committees. These meet on a regular basis. Other committees are formed from time to time to deal with specific issues. These are called standing committees and they usually meet for a limited time. Committees make reports to the House of Commons.

The Cabinet

The Cabinet is a group of senior ministers who meet to decide the government's policy on issues and events. It also decides how issues will be dealt with and who will take the lead on important events.

A cabinet meeting

Leading members of the Cabinet include:

- the Deputy Prime Minister
- the Chancellor of the Exchequer, who is responsible for the country's finance
- the Home Secretary, who is in charge of home affairs including the police force and keeping law and order
- the Foreign Secretary, who is responsible for relations with foreign countries
- the Secretary of State for Education, who is responsible for the state education system, its teachers and their performance
- senior ministers with responsibility for health, transport, defence, the environment, etc.

(A) Activities

1 Look at the House of Commons website. Find details of three bills that are being considered by Parliament.

2 Find out the names of the five members of the Cabinet listed above.

The House of Lords

The upper chamber of the Houses of Parliament is the House of Lords, which has existed since the 1300s. It is made up of

- archbishops and bishops
- life peers (lords) representing political parties, independent peers and hereditary peers.

Reforms of the House of Lords are being prepared for discussion by Parliament.

The House of Lords has many functions.

- It debates issues of national importance which are not debated by the House of Commons.
- It considers bills which have been passed through the reading stages of the House of Commons and suggests ways in which they can be changed.
- It is the final court of appeal in the UK. The 26 law lords of the House of Lords have the final judgement on any case that they are required to consider. The law lords have the power to go against a decision of the High Court – they are the highest power in the British system.

The State opening of Parliament

The European Union

The European Union (EU) is made up of fifteen countries known as the member states. To be a member of the EU, countries must make sure that:

- their system of government is democratic

- they respect human rights

- they operate a market economy (see page 32) which matches the economies of existing EU member states.

The EU is run by five main institutions along with the European Council. The European Council is a summit meeting of the heads of government from each member state. These meetings are usually held twice a year. The European Council decides policy.

The five institutions of the EU are:

- The Council of Ministers

- The European Commission

- The European Parliament

- The European Court of Justice

- The European Court of Auditors.

The European Economic Community (EEC) was formed in 1957 by six countries. It was a common market where labour, goods and services could be freely traded. The United Kingdom joined the EEC in 1973. The EEC became the EU when the single market came into being in 1993. The single currency (the euro) was introduced into thirteen EU countries in 2002.

The Council of Ministers

This is the main decision-making body of the EU. It is made up of one representative of each member state. The UK is represented by the foreign secretary. Decisions are made by voting. Any country has the right to stop a decision that would not be good for the country.

The European Commission

The European Commission is based in Brussels. Its main functions are:

- suggesting policies and drafting laws

- making sure that member states keep to EU treaties and policies

- managing the administration of the EU.

The EU has 20 commissioners and over 10 000 staff. Each country can appoint one commissioner. France, Spain, Germany, Italy and the UK have two commissioners. Commissioners specialize in different areas of EU policy.

(A) Activities

1 Find the names of the fifteen member states of the EU.

2 Why do you think less than 50 per cent of people vote at European elections? Talk about the reasons for this.

3 Do you think that it is fair to set rules for entry to the EU? What do you think would happen if the poorer countries of Europe were allowed to join the EU?

The European Parliament

The European Parliament meets in Strasbourg and Brussels. Representatives are called Members of the European Parliament (MEPs) and are elected to serve for a maximum of five years. Elections for the 626 MEPs are held in June. Since 1999 MEPs have been elected using proportional representation. MEPs represent a constituency which is larger in area than a national government constituency.

The European Parliament:

- makes decisions on the suggestions put forward by the European Commission

- makes sure that trade is fairly spread across Europe

- makes sure that laws are fair to all member states

- is funded through contributions from member states.

The EU Parliament building

The European Court of Justice

The European Court of Justice is in Luxembourg. It has fifteen judges, one from each member country. The court sits to consider disputes about EU laws. Its function is to sort out disputes, and to decide on how EU law should be followed. The European Court of Justice has the power to rule against a decision of a national government.

The European Court of Auditors

This organization monitors the financial management of the EU. Its main function is to make sure that the EU's finance is being used for the purposes for which it was raised. It also helps the EU Parliament to check its annual budget spending. The Court of Auditors is made up of fifteen members, one from each country.

 Activities

1 Find out the names of the two British European Commissioners.

2 Who is the MEP representing your area? Which MEP constituency do you live in?

3 Find out the address of your MEP from the European Union website. Write to your MEP to ask what he or she is trying to do for your constituency.

Visit the European Union website at www.heinemann.co.uk/hotlinks

Taking part in the democratic process

Elections

Who can vote?

Every year your local council will make a new register of electors. You must be eighteen to vote. The register tells the returning officer who is allowed to vote in an election. Members of the House of Lords and convicted prisoners are not allowed to vote. All men over the age of 21 have been allowed to vote since 1884. Women over the age of 21 were not given the right to vote until 1928.

How to vote

When an election is called, the returning officer will contact each voter and invite them to vote at a polling station between set hours on the day of the election. The polling station will be managed by polling clerks who will make sure

Taking part – voting

that everyone's vote is kept secret. This is called a secret ballot. Each voter receives a specially stamped ballot paper on which to vote. The ballot paper names all of the candidates who are standing for election and the political parties which they represent. Voters put a cross beside the candidate they are voting for.

Who can be a candidate?

Candidates standing for election must be 21 years of age and British citizens. The following people cannot stand for election:

- members of the Anglican or Roman Catholic clergy
- members of the House of Lords
- civil servants
- judges
- members of the armed services
- police officers.

Candidates have to be nominated by ten people who live in the constituency. Candidates are required to pay the returning officer a deposit of £500, which is lost if a candidate fails to win 5 per cent of the vote at the election.

Why do we vote?

One of the benefits of a democracy is that the people are involved in choosing who will govern. We also choose the political party whose manifesto most meets our needs. The turnout at local, national and European elections is falling. Some people think that this is because people:

- think all politicians are the same
- don't like the present system
- don't have confidence in the present system.

Figure 4.2

(A) Activities

1 Would you like to be an MP? Give reasons for your answer.

2 Find out the most recent local election results for your ward of the council. Compare the results for the candidates of different parties.

3 Find the general election results for your constituency for 1997 and 2001. Why do you think the results for the two years are different?

4 You are a candidate in an election. Prepare a poster to include:

- what you believe in
- why you should be elected.

Every democracy tries to get its people involved by giving them information so they can make decisions. Politicians from all political parties accept that there is a need for all people to be involved in the political system. They think that all parties should try to increase the number of people who vote in elections. At present, most MPs are middle-aged, male and white. Parliament is not representative of the ethnic or gender balance in the country. There has been some improvement in recent years, but much remains to be done.

In recent years fewer young people have voted at general elections. The major political parties have asked personalities and pop stars to help them encourage young people to vote.

Referenda

Sometimes there is an issue of national importance that will affect people's lives. In instances like this a referendum may be held. Britain held a referendum in 1975 to decide whether or not to continue as a member of the Common Market. Some countries, such as Switzerland, use referenda far more regularly than other countries, as they want to know how the citizens of the country feel about important issues.

People who support the use of referenda have argued that this system gives more power to the ordinary people by allowing them to make decisions about issues which affect their lives. People who are against referenda have argued that the system is expensive. They also think we should let MPs make decisions as we have elected them to represent us.

To increase the number of people voting, some areas have allowed voters to vote by post.

1975 Referendum poster

Referenda are worded as questions. It is important that the question is asked in a straightforward way or the result could be confused. A question worded in a certain way might influence the way people vote.

Using the Internet

Some people think that the Internet should be used to ask the public what they think about issues which affect them. They think that this would be a quick and efficient way of finding out people's views. Other people argue that it is useful as a research tool to find out what people think about issues, but that it would be unfair on those who are not able to use the Internet.

Local council consultation

Local councils have started to ask residents what they think about important issues like new housing, road developments or changes to the education system. They invite them to meetings or send them documents for comment. Local people are often kept informed about the workings of their local council through local council news magazines.

(A) Activities

1 Find out what issues your local council has asked people for their views on in the past year.

2 How does your local council keep you informed?

3 Do you think referenda are a good way of getting more people involved in making decisions? Talk about this in groups.

4 If you were holding a referendum about drinking at the age of sixteen, how would you word the question you asked on the ballot paper?

How national government manages the economy

The government has to raise money to finance public spending. This is the money spent on health, education, defence, police and prisons, housing and other public services. The government raises its money through a system of taxation:

Direct taxation – Some taxes are raised through the income people earn. The rate of taxation changes according to how much a person earns. Generally, the more money they earn, the more tax they pay. The government raises most of its money through income tax.

Indirect taxation – Value added tax (VAT) is an indirect tax. This does not depend on what people earn. It is set at a fixed rate and is charged on goods and services. The person who sells the product or service adds the tax to the price, then pays the VAT to the government.

Proportional tax – This stays at the same percentage regardless of how much people earn. National Insurance contributions are a proportional tax. These contributions are used to fund social security payments such as the state pension. There will be major changes to this area of taxation in the future.

The budget

Each year the government makes a statement about the levels of taxation for the coming year and the allowances for children, family and older people. This is known as the budget. The Chancellor of the Exchequer makes the budget statement to the House of Commons, usually in March. The budget statement gives the government's plans for spending for the next year.

The way the government chooses to raise finance and spend its money will have an effect

Figure 4.3

on how people live. If the government raises direct taxation and raises VAT on goods, then people will have less money to spend and save. By far the greatest amount of money spent by the government is on social security. This includes unemployment benefits, income support and pensions.

The government needs to increase state benefits regularly or many unemployed, disabled and ill people will find it difficult to pay bills and stay healthy. Balancing the books and keeping the country safe and happy while caring for the sick and the disabled are some of the issues facing government.

Inflation

One of the measures used by the government in setting targets is the level of inflation. This refers to the amount by which the price of goods has increased in the past year. If the price of food has increased by 3 per cent in the last year, then the inflation for food will be 3 per cent.

The government sets targets for inflation to keep inflation under control. If inflation is high, everyday goods become too expensive for ordinary people. If inflation is low, the economy might slow down, leading to job losses and less spending money. It is important that the government gets its targets for inflation right.

Government spending

There are fifteen main government departments which rely on public money to function. Each year the government decides how much money will be spent in each department. The government decided in 1998 to set out a three-year spending plan. Typical government spending is shown in Figure 4.4.

Education	12%
Social security	32%
Health and related services	17%
Housing, environment, heritage	5%
Industry, agriculture, employment	4%
Defence	7%
Law and order	5%
Transport	3%
Debt interest	8%
Other expenditure	7%

Figure 4.4 Typical government spending

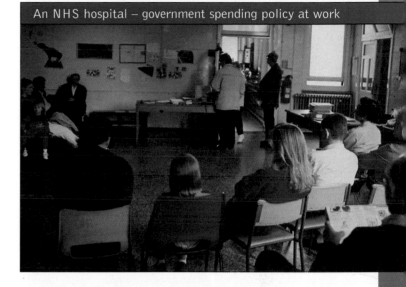
An NHS hospital – government spending policy at work

Controlling government spending

The House of Commons has a duty to make sure that the government does not raise money through taxation without good cause. The budget proposals are presented to the House of Commons as a Finance Bill. It takes about four months for the bill to pass through the stages (see page 87) to become a Finance Act, allowing the government to raise the money it needs. In this way the proposals for raising finance are discussed fully and examined carefully. A select committee, known as the Public Accounts Committee, meets and examines the accounts of each department to check that the money is being spent on the programmes for which it was raised.

The Chancellor Gordon Brown on budget day

Becoming a European citizen

The single currency

Britain joined the EEC in 1973. All three major political parties broadly agree with the single market and Britain's membership of the EU. There is disagreement about Britain joining the single currency.

All EU countries qualify for membership of the single currency, although Britain and Denmark have chosen not to introduce the euro. The euro became the currency of the other thirteen members of the EU in 2002. Although not used in the UK, the euro is accepted in some UK shops, for example Marks and Spencer.

People who support the UK joining the single currency say that it will make buying and selling in Europe easier because every country will have the same currency. If there is no cost for changing money from one currency into another, costs for business would fall. This could lead to the creation of more jobs.

Those people against the single currency say that the economy of different countries will not be able to grow at different rates. This is because the euro has the same value throughout Europe. They also think that Britain will be less British without the pound and worry that more decisions about Britain's finances will be made by Europe.

(A) Activities

1 If you were in charge of the budget what would your spending priorities be? Choose three and explain why you think they are important. What does the whole group think is important?

2 Which method of taxation do you think is fairer – direct taxes or indirect taxes? Talk about this in a group.

The euro

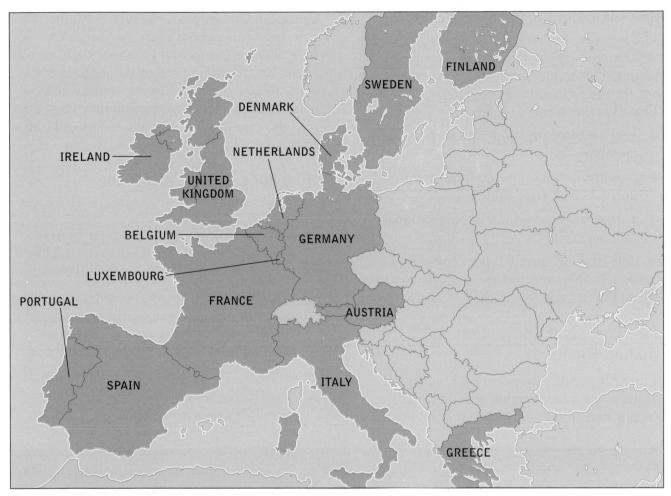

Figure 4.5 The fifteen member states of the European Union

The EU budget

The budget for the EU is set each year by the European Parliament and the Council of Ministers. An example of EU income is shown in Figure 4.6.

Customs duties	15%
VAT	42%
Contributions from member countries	40%
Taxes on agricultural products	3%

Figure 4.6 EU income

Some countries such as Greece, Ireland and Portugal receive more from the EU than they contribute. The UK and Germany put more money in than they take out. They are known as 'net contributors' to the EU budget.

An example of EU spending is shown in Figure 4.7.

Fisheries, farms, infrastructure, regional and social affairs	35.5%
Agriculture	46%
Administration	5%
Overseas aid	6.5%
Research and technology	4%
Miscellaneous	3%

Figure 4.7 EU spending

How much does EU membership cost?

The member states of the EU each give some of their country's money to the European Union. This money is given to EU countries to pay for the EU's agreed programme of action. The EU takes a share of the:

- VAT charged on goods and services in member states
- customs duties on goods imported from non-EU countries, and
- a share of each country's gross national product (GNP).

In 1993, the UK gave 0.9 per cent of its GNP to the EU. This means that every person paid about 37p per day to the EU.

The European Convention on Human Rights

The European Convention on Human Rights protects the human rights of individuals or groups in Europe. This work is done by the European Commission of Human Rights. The commission is elected every six years. Any individual or group who feels that their human rights have been ignored or damaged in some way can take their case to the commission for consideration. The commission may choose to pass the case to the European Court of Human Rights for a judgement.

How does the EU affect the average citizen?

- As a citizen of the EU, it is easier to travel, work and study in Europe than it would be if the UK was not a member of the EU.
- The European Commission of Human Rights makes sure that human rights are protected in all EU countries. Good human rights are required before a country can become a member of the EU.
- The EU has a set of rules which apply to consumer goods across the EU.

The Eurostar makes it easier to travel to Europe

- Food labelling and safety regulations for toys and electrical goods must be followed by all member states.

- The EU gives funds for projects in poorer regions of Europe.

- The EU has developed programmes to improve the environment. These include
  - cutting air pollution
  - encouraging the use of public transport
  - setting basic water and bathing standards on beaches
  - cutting down on noise in the community and the workplace
  - getting rid of nuclear materials and chemicals safely
  - creating environmentally sensitive areas to protect forests and wildlife.

European bathing standards at work

 Activities

1 Do you think that the UK should stay a part of the EU? Give reasons for your answer.

2 Do you think the UK should join the single currency? Why?

3 With a partner, talk about why it is better for Britain to be part of Europe.

4 Name three things the EU has done to help its citizens.

Trade and the EU

In 1994, the European Economic Area (EEA) was created. This included members of the EU and other countries in Europe. It was formed to strengthen the free trade links between European countries and the rest of the world. When dealing with big trading partners such as Japan or the USA, the EU gets a better price for goods than one country would get on its own.

Young Germans, protesting against transportation of nuclear waste

Check it out

What you should have learned from this chapter

Look at the areas of study in the table. You should now know and understand the language and ideas that we have explored in Chapter 4: National and European government.

The activities and questions in the chapter, and the extra sheets your teacher will have worked through with you, should have helped you to learn about this topic.

If some of the areas are not clear, read through the pages again. If you are still not sure, ask your teacher to explain them again.

Areas of study	Page
Understanding how the UK is governed	62–63
Political parties	64
How national government works	64–66
The institutions of the European Union	67–68
How and why we vote	69–70
The budget and taxation	72
Government spending	73
How the EU works	75–76
Becoming a European citizen	74
Trade and the EU	77

You should be able to answer all the following questions. These are short answer questions similar to those that will appear in Section A of the written exam paper that you will sit at the end of the course.

The knowledge and ideas covered in this chapter will also be tested in longer, more detailed questions in Sections B and D of the exam paper.

1 Name the five institutions of the EU.

2 Where does the European Parliament meet?

3 List the functions of the European Commission.

4 What is a democracy?

5 Explain the difference between a referendum and an election.

6 What is a register of electors?

7 What system is used to elect MEPs?

8 Name three political parties in the UK.

9 What are taxes?

10 What is the European Economic Area (EEA)?

11 Which committee monitors government spending?

5 Criminal and civil law

How does the law affect you?

As a child you only have a few rights under the law. As you get older the law requires you to do more things for yourself and to accept responsibility for your own actions. Figure 5.1 shows what you can do at certain ages.

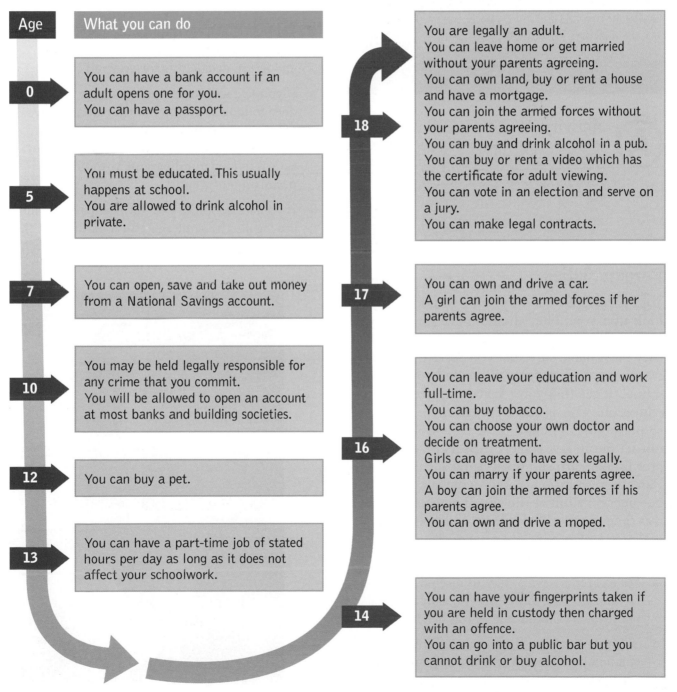

Age	What you can do
0	You can have a bank account if an adult opens one for you. You can have a passport.
5	You must be educated. This usually happens at school. You are allowed to drink alcohol in private.
7	You can open, save and take out money from a National Savings account.
10	You may be held legally responsible for any crime that you commit. You will be allowed to open an account at most banks and building societies.
12	You can buy a pet.
13	You can have a part-time job of stated hours per day as long as it does not affect your schoolwork.
14	You can have your fingerprints taken if you are held in custody then charged with an offence. You can go into a public bar but you cannot drink or buy alcohol.
16	You can leave your education and work full-time. You can buy tobacco. You can choose your own doctor and decide on treatment. Girls can agree to have sex legally. You can marry if your parents agree. A boy can join the armed forces if his parents agree. You can own and drive a moped.
17	You can own and drive a car. A girl can join the armed forces if her parents agree.
18	You are legally an adult. You can leave home or get married without your parents agreeing. You can own land, buy or rent a house and have a mortgage. You can join the armed forces without your parents agreeing. You can buy and drink alcohol in a pub. You can buy or rent a video which has the certificate for adult viewing. You can vote in an election and serve on a jury. You can make legal contracts.

Figure 5.1 What the law allows you to do, from age 0–18

Delivering papers earns this 13-year-old money *and* leaves time for school

Ⓐ Activity

Why do you think a person's rights are different according to how old they are? For example, why must you be 12 years old to buy a pet?

Parents' duties

Your parents have a duty and a responsibility to look after you. They should make sure that you are properly fed and clothed. If you are ill, then they must make sure that you receive medical treatment. Your parents must send you to school or see that you receive a proper education. This is known as parental responsibility. Though these responsibilities are not set out in law, society expects parents to give proper care and protection to children. Parental responsibility ends when a child becomes an adult at the age of eighteen. From this time parents advise their children.

Facts about life at home

- Your parents have a duty to discipline you and can decide how to punish you. Any physical punishment should not be too harsh.

- Your parents have the right to decide how you will be educated and which school you will go to.

- Your parents will decide which doctor and dentist you will see and which treatment you need.

- If your parents split up, a court will decide who you will live with. The court will take your views into account.

- If your parents split up, you have the right to have contact with both parents unless a court rules against this.

- Your parents have the right to decide which religion you will follow until you are old enough to decide this for yourself.

- If you live with foster parents, they have a duty to look after you but they do not have the rights of your natural parents. A child who has been fostered for five years cannot return to its natural parents without the permission of a court.

- If you are adopted, you get new parents who are legally the same as natural parents. At the age of eighteen you have the right to see a copy of your original birth certificate.

This little girl's first day at school

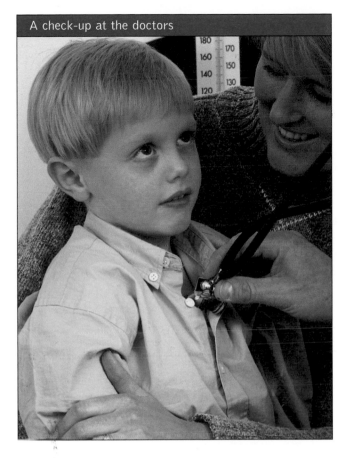

A check-up at the doctors

Activity

A

Talk about the following four statements:

- Children should be allowed to choose their own medical treatment from the age of twelve.

- Children should choose their secondary school.

- Smacking is a good way to discipline children.

- All children should receive £5 pocket money per week at eleven years of age.

Say why you agree or disagree with them.

Breakdown in standards of care

If parents do not care for their children properly or if they neglect or are cruel to them, then they may be taken to court. The court will decide what to do. It may decide to take the children from their parents and give the power to decide on their care to someone else. Care is usually given to the local authority, but it could be given to a family member. The parents may be allowed to keep control of the children's care with checks on their behaviour.

If a child is taken into local authority care, the local authority will look at his or her needs. He or she may go to live in a children's home or with foster parents. The law tries to take the wishes of the child into account. Social workers, doctors and carers will try to do what is best for the child.

Consumers and the law

A consumer is someone who buys goods and services. A consumer makes an agreement with the person selling the goods. This agreement is a contract in law. Your rights as a consumer are laid down in laws such as:

- the Trade Descriptions Act 1968

- the Sale of Goods Act 1979

- the supply of Goods and Services Act 1982.

The Office of Fair Trading will give advice and information on consumer issues. Problems can be referred to a Local Authority Trading Standards Department.

The EU and the consumer

With the free movement of goods in the EU, consumers have a far wider choice. European producers have to make sure that all products are safe and meet the minimum hygiene and quality standards. The EU has rulings on:

- toys
- packaging for household appliances
- labelling
- hygiene for food processing.

The EU brought in protection against unfair selling practices and travelling problems. Consumers are given a 'cooling-off' period of one week when they can decide not to purchase any item if the sale was negotiated at home. People on holiday also have the right to compensation, for example if a holiday is cancelled.

Street trading

i

The Supply of Goods and Services Act 1982 – the person providing a service must have the necessary skills. They must provide the service within a reasonable timescale. The price paid for the service must be agreed in advance.

The Sale of Goods Act 1979 – goods must be of 'merchantable quality', fit for the purpose and described in full by the seller, by display or on the package. This law covers goods wherever they are bought – on the doorstep, from a street trader, by mail order or from a shop. It applies to sale items and special offers, though consumers should expect goods marked as 'seconds' to be of poorer quality. If goods are broken or faulty, the seller is responsible for the goods and should arrange for a refund or exchange.

The Trades Descriptions Act 1968 – it is an offence for a shopkeeper or trader to knowingly give a false description of the goods or services which they supply or of the use to which the goods can be put. Any problems should be referred to a Trading Standards Officer.

(A) Activities

1 Write to the Trading Standards Officer at your local council to find out how they check on local businesses.

2 Watch the programme *Watchdog* and list some of the consumer stories which they investigate on behalf of the general public. For each story you list, write down:
   - the name of the company
   - what the problem is
   - what action *Watchdog* takes
   - what happens as a result of *Watchdog's* actions.

Young people and employment

The law for young people in employment changes at different ages. In all cases there is a requirement that any employment will not interfere with schoolwork. A young person should have the permission of their school before taking on employment.

Information about the number of hours young people can work at each age is available from the local careers office or an Educational Welfare Officer. Young people can work full-time at the age of sixteen and can do part-time work from the age of thirteen. They can work for up to two hours on a school day or a Sunday and longer on a Saturday. They can only work between 7 am and 7 pm. No employer can ask them to do any job which involves heavy lifting or moving which could cause injury.

Working for a living

Activities

A

1 Get a copy of the employment regulations for young people from your local careers office. Talk about whether you think these are fair.

2 How many of the young people you know who work break these regulations? Why do you think this happens?

The law and discrimination

The law gives everyone equal rights. Laws protect people from discrimination on the grounds of race, sex or disability. Proving discrimination can be difficult. It is necessary to prove that the actions of an individual, group of individuals or institution led to less favourable treatment and that discrimination was the result.

Types of discrimination

Direct discrimination is when a person is treated less favourably than someone else doing the same job. This might refer to pay, career opportunities or number of hours worked.

Indirect discrimination is when the conditions required for a job cannot be applied equally to all people. For example, if a company only employs people who take a size 43 shoe or above, it may be discriminating against women.

Protecting people – The Social Chapter

The Social Chapter is a charter of rights for workers. It was felt that many groups of people in the workplace did not have the same rights as permanent full-time workers and that

Racial discrimination

The Race Relations Act 1976 aims to prevent racial discrimination. It makes it illegal to discriminate on the grounds of ethnic origin or colour in matters relating to employment, education, housing, and the provision of goods and services. It is an offence under the Public Order Act to encourage any activity that is likely to lead to racial hatred.

Sex discrimination

The Sex Discrimination Acts 1975 and 1986 state that it is unlawful to treat a person less favourably than a person of the opposite sex. Care should be taken when a job is advertised to choose wording which makes sure that both males and females are encouraged to apply. The Act also states that services provided in the community should be of the same standard when offered to males and females. It is unlawful to offer poorer services to one group.

Disability discrimination

It is illegal to discriminate against someone with a disability in matters relating to employment, education, housing, public services and public transport. **The 1995 Disability Discrimination Act** strengthened the rights of people in employment. A firm cannot discriminate when recruiting, training, promoting and dismissing. In addition, employers must make changes to the workplace that would enable a person with a disability to do the job. If it can be proved that an employer has not followed the Act, this would be discrimination. The Act applies to firms with 20 or more employees.

something needed to be done for these groups of people. The aim was to improve the living and working conditions of EU citizens. These rights included:

- employment rights for part-time and temporary workers

- the right to annual paid holiday and to daily and weekly minimum rest periods for daytime and night work

- the right for men and women to have equal treatment – equal pay for equal work

- protection for pregnant women and nursing mothers, the right to a minimum period of leave, time off for medical examinations and job protection while pregnant

- the right to health and safety protection including protective clothing and first-aid facilities

- better employment opportunities for disabled people and easier access to the workplace.

Equal opportunity at work

Activity

Write to your local Citizens Advice Bureau or Law Centre and ask for information about discrimination. Talk about how the information helps people who feel they have been discriminated against.

What is crime?

A crime is an act that is unlawful or illegal. It is an offence against the law of the land. There are two main types of crime:

- crimes against people, such as assault and murder
- crimes against property, such as vandalism and arson.

Attitudes to crime have changed over the years. In the nineteenth century it was possible to be put in prison for stealing bread. Today the punishment would probably be a fine. What is a crime in Britain may not be a crime somewhere else. For example, in Holland, smoking cannabis in public is allowed, but it is not allowed in Britain.

Some people believe that the increase in crime is connected to people wanting to possess more things. Others think that it is connected to factors such as the breakdown of families and lower moral standards due to fewer people having religious beliefs, unemployment, films and television programmes about crime and criminals, or drinking and drug-taking.

Guarding against crime

The police force is the public's front-line defence against crime and criminals. The main duties of the police force are:

- to prevent and detect crime
- to protect life and property
- to keep public order.

The police force needs the support of the public to undertake its duties efficiently. A major part of these duties is to ask questions and to search property. The Police and Criminal Evidence Act 1984 sets out the police duties and powers.

A police officer working with the community

The police have the power to stop people and search them in certain situations. If you are stopped by a police officer you should

- ask their name and the police station where they work
- ask why you have been stopped
- give your name and address.

You do not have to answer any questions at this stage.

The police can search you after you have been arrested or if you are suspected of carrying:

- anything that could be used for a burglary or theft
- stolen goods
- drugs
- weapons, or anything that could be used as a weapon.

The officer should explain why you are being searched and what they expect to find.

Activities

1   Some people believe that the power to stop and search is used too much. Other people think that the police should be able to stop and search at random. Talk about this in groups.

2   Look at the main duties of the police on page 85. What would happen if there was no police force to carry them out? Talk this over in pairs.

3   The police are our protectors. Do you agree with this statement? Write five sentences about this.

Helping the police

Everyone should be prepared to help the police to keep law and order. This helps the public to feel safe. If you are asked to help the police, you have the right to refuse, but if the police arrest you, you must go with them.

At the police station:

- you have the right to send a message to a friend or family member
- you have the right to advice from a solicitor
- if you are under sixteen, you cannot be questioned without a parent or adult being present
- you must give your name and address
- you do not have to answer any questions.

Helping the police with their enquiries does not always mean that the person being questioned is accused of the offence.

A police officer at the station's front desk

Being arrested

If you have been arrested and charged with an offence, you may be:

- reprimanded, or given a warning or caution. A police officer talks to you about the offence and explains what will happen if you break the law again. The police will keep a record of the crime. Only people who have admitted they have broken the law can be reprimanded or cautioned. If you have committed three offences, you will automatically face prosecution for the third offence.

- prosecuted. Your case will be referred to court for consideration. If you are found guilty and sentenced, you will have a criminal record.

Police records

The police collect a wide range of information on people. The information is stored on the Police National Computer. The information is available at every police station. If you are between the ages of ten and seventeen, the police will hold a record of your crime until you are seventeen. If you are over seventeen, the record will be held for five years if you are reprimanded or charged with a recordable offence.

Checking up on the police

The Police and Criminal Evidence Act has guidelines which make sure that the police act within the law. Officers will be disciplined if they:

- neglect their duty
- make a false statement
- treat people badly
- are rude or insulting to a member of the public
- show racial discrimination.

Anyone who wishes to complain about the police can get information from the Police Complaints Authority.

Law-making in action

As we have already learned, one of the main jobs of the House of Commons is to make the laws of the land. Laws are made so everyone is governed by the same set of rules. This makes life easier for everyone.

Before a law is made, it must go through a long process in Parliament. For a law to be made it has to be put before Parliament as a bill. The bill has to go through a number of stages before it is made into a law. These stages are shown in Figure 5.2.

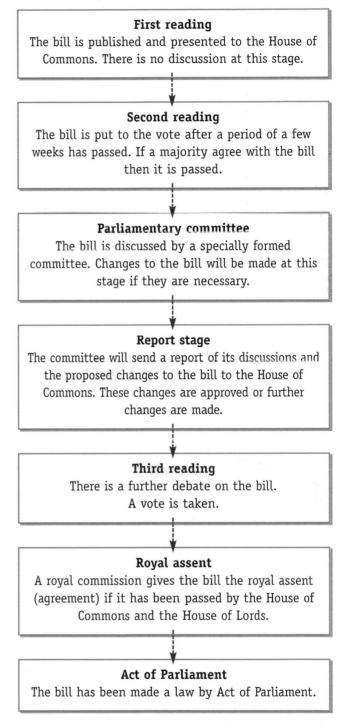

First reading
The bill is published and presented to the House of Commons. There is no discussion at this stage.

Second reading
The bill is put to the vote after a period of a few weeks has passed. If a majority agree with the bill then it is passed.

Parliamentary committee
The bill is discussed by a specially formed committee. Changes to the bill will be made at this stage if they are necessary.

Report stage
The committee will send a report of its discussions and the proposed changes to the bill to the House of Commons. These changes are approved or further changes are made.

Third reading
There is a further debate on the bill.
A vote is taken.

Royal assent
A royal commission gives the bill the royal assent (agreement) if it has been passed by the House of Commons and the House of Lords.

Act of Parliament
The bill has been made a law by Act of Parliament.

Figure 5.2 How laws are made

To become an Act of Parliament a bill must pass through all the stages shown in Figure 5.2 in both the House of Commons and the House of Lords. Most bills are passed with agreement between the Houses of Parliament.

Activities

1   Explain the difference between a bill and an Act of Parliament.

2   School rules are made to help everyone at school have equal rights. Which of your school rules would you change? Why?

Types of law in Britain

Laws in Britain have been made over the years in a variety of ways.

- **Statutes** are laws that have been made by Parliament.

- **Common law** includes laws that have been passed down through the ages. Everyone knew these laws and the courts based their decisions upon them.

- **Bylaws** are made by local councils and some public agencies. They deal with local matters such as litter, dog fouling or other anti-social behaviour.

When laws are passed, it is up to the legal system to put them into practice. If a case is presented to court for a decision, the judge will investigate other cases to see if there has been a similar case in the past. The judge's decision will be based on the previous cases. This is known as case law.

Judges, on their way to court

European laws

The European government also makes laws (Figure 5.3).

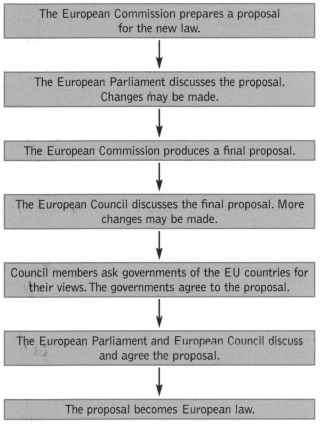

Figure 5.3 How European laws are made

European laws apply to all member countries. They are known as regulations. Sometimes the European Union will issue a 'directive' to member countries. The directive will instruct member states to introduce the new law within a set time limit.

How does European law become UK law?

European law is made into national law in the Houses of Parliament. Proposals from the European Commission are sent to London and discussed by senior civil servants. At the same time the proposals will be discussed by the civil servants representing the governments of the EU countries in Brussels. The proposals will be considered by the UK's minister for Europe and select committees in the House of Lords and the House of Commons. Finally the proposals are presented to Parliament for consideration.

I'll see you in court!

In Britain, there are two types of law:

- Civil law relates to people's private rights, for example arguments about the boundaries of people's property and marriage breakdown.

- Criminal law relates to crimes which are against the law of the land.

Each set of laws is heard in its own court system. Each court has its own way of operating.

Figure 5.4

Civil law

Because civil law relates to disputes concerning agreements with another person over a private matter, the matter is often dealt with by a solicitor without going to court. These cases are said to have been settled 'out of court'. If the case is sent to court, sometimes a solicitor can act on your behalf so you don't have to be present.

Dealing with civil cases

Civil cases are considered in county courts. In these cases one person takes action against another. We call the person taking the action 'the plaintiff' and the person against whom the action is being taken 'the defendant'. For example, in the cartoon on page 89, the man who is complaining that the boundary has been moved would be the plaintiff in court. The man who is putting the fence up would be the defendant. If the court decides that the defendant is acting against the law, the court will make a judgement. The defendant usually has to pay 'damages' to the plaintiff, which are a form of compensation. The defendant may appeal against a court decision.

County courts deal with contracts up to a certain sum, straightforward divorces, small

A county court

claims of less than £5000 and other civil issues. In county courts the cases are heard by a judge.

A higher level of civil court deals with larger issues (see Figure 5.5). If a person feels that they were not dealt with fairly they may appeal against the decision. The issue would be referred to the Court of Appeal. The final appeal could be referred to the House of Lords if it was considered to be of public importance.

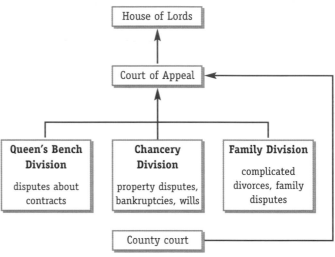

Figure 5.5 The different civil courts

Criminal law

Criminal law relates to matters such as theft, assault, rape, drug offences, violence and murder. The aim of a prosecution is to punish the offender, if that person is found guilty. The law sets out the punishment to be given.

Dealing with criminal cases

Most cases of criminal law are heard in magistrates' courts. Sometimes a magistrates' court will send a case to the crown court. Most towns have a magistrates' court so they usually deal with local cases.

Magistrates' courts are held by magistrates or 'justices of the peace' (JPs). JPs work unpaid. Cases are heard by a bench of magistrates. If the person is found guilty, magistrates will decide on a sentence from a set range of sentences for the crime committed. The magistrates have no legal training so are supported on matters of law by a clerk of court.

Trial by jury

When a case is held at a crown court it is heard by a judge and jury (see page 92). Usually the defendant has pleaded not guilty. When a defendant pleads guilty the judge decides on the sentence immediately.

Figure 5.6 shows what happens during a trial. The barrister speaking for the plaintiff is called the prosecution. The barrister speaking for the defendant is called the defence.

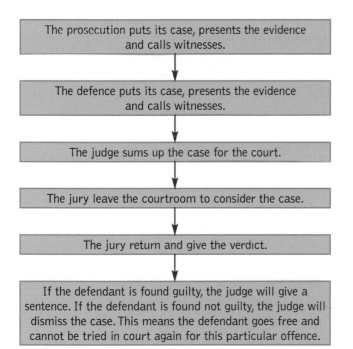

The prosecution puts its case, presents the evidence and calls witnesses.

↓

The defence puts its case, presents the evidence and calls witnesses.

↓

The judge sums up the case for the court.

↓

The jury leave the courtroom to consider the case.

↓

The jury return and give the verdict.

↓

If the defendant is found guilty, the judge will give a sentence. If the defendant is found not guilty, the judge will dismiss the case. This means the defendant goes free and cannot be tried in court again for this particular offence.

Figure 5.6 What happens during a trial

The rights of accused people

In the British legal system, a person accused of a crime has rights set down in law. These rights apply to every case.

- A person is assumed innocent until it has been proved they are guilty.

- Except in youth court cases (see page 92), the case will be heard in public.

- The court has a duty to listen to the accused and his/her lawyer as long as what they are saying is relevant to the defence of the case.

- Witnesses must give evidence in the presence of the accused. The accused has the right to ask questions of the witnesses after they have completed their evidence.

The central criminal court – statue of Justice on the Old Bailey dome, London

- Proof of the crime the accused is supposed to have committed must be beyond all reasonable doubt.

- The prosecution must prove the charge against the accused.

- Once a person has been tried and a decision has been reached on whether the person is guilty, the person cannot be charged with that particular offence again.

People in the legal system

Judges

Judges must be qualified barristers or solicitors and are appointed to the job by the Lord Chancellor. Judges do not yet represent our society as they are mainly middle-class, white and male. They are paid for their work.

Solicitors and barristers

People who work in the law in England and Wales are either solicitors or barristers. There are many more solicitors in practice than barristers.

Solicitors work with people who may need legal advice about:

- claims following an accident
- problems in a marriage
- tax problems
- laws about land they own
- buying or selling a house
- making a will
- crime
- business problems.

Solicitors may work in private practice, for public organizations or in industry.

A barrister is a specialist in advocacy, which is the presentation of the client's case to the court which has to decide it. Barristers need to have a detailed knowledge of the law, good judgement and the ability to present a case clearly. They will prepare every case thoroughly.

A barrister will also act on behalf of the Crown Prosecution Service (see opposite) in court.

Activities

1 Try to arrange to visit the public gallery of a court. Make notes about what happens.

2 Is it always necessary to have trial by jury? Judges could hear cases and make a judgement without a jury. What do you think is the best way?

Jury

A jury is selected randomly from the current electoral register. Twelve adults between the ages of 18 and 70 make up a jury. The following people cannot sit on a jury:

- those who have been to prison in the last ten years
- those who have been on probation in the last five years
- ministers of religion
- lawyers
- police officers.

Crown Prosecution Service

People who commit crimes are prosecuted by the crown, that is the state. Before 1986, prosecutions were brought by the police. The Crown Prosecution Service (CPS) decides which cases to prosecute. It is led by the Director of Public Prosecutions.

Youth courts

Children under the age of ten cannot be charged with a criminal offence. Children under sixteen must be accompanied by a parent when their case is heard in court. All cases where the person charged is under eighteen are heard in a youth court unless it is a serious offence. Serious offences are often heard in a crown court.

Members of the public are not allowed into a youth court and the defendant must not be named in any press coverage. Magistrates who consider youth cases are specially trained to deal with the issues in a more informal manner.

Activities

1 What are the main differences between a magistrates' court and a youth court?

2 Do youth courts make it too easy for the accused person? Talk about this in groups.

The European Court

The European Court of Justice was set up in 1952. It deals with more than 400 cases a year. The Court of First Instance was set up in 1989 to help the European Court of Justice.

The Court of Justice has fifteen judges and eight barristers. The Court of First Instance has fifteen judges. In both courts cases are heard by a panel of three to five judges.

What are its powers

It is the responsibility of the European Court of Justice to make sure that the law (of the EU) is kept in the member states. If EU law is relevant to a case being heard in a national court of one of the EU countries, the Court of Justice tells the national court which EU law it must follow. The Court of Justice deals with cases relating to:

- going against the treaty which EU countries agreed to

- damages (money given as compensation for a loss or injury)

- not keeping to decisions made by the European Council

- decisions on what the European law means

- appeals against judgements of the Court of First Instance.

Inside the European Court of Justice

The Court of First Instance has the power to rule at the first court hearing on:

- requests from member states for parts of laws to be removed

- cases brought against the commission under the Treaty

- disputes between the EU and its officials and workers.

More information on the European Court and how it works, and also on how the European Court affects the lives of its citizens, can be found at:

www.heinemann.co.uk/hotlinks

Case study: Criminal law – robbery

We often hear how elderly people are beaten and robbed. Here is Harry's story.

Robbery of an elderly man

Harry is an 84-year-old retired welder who lives in a bungalow in a warden-controlled complex on the outskirts of a small town. Harry is a widower. His two daughters live in the town with their families. All of the people in this small cul-de-sac are elderly and they rely on each other and their warden for support in times of distress.

One cold night in December, Harry had a heavy cold and was finding it difficult to sleep. He was watching News 24 on television at about 3.30 am when there was a knock on the door. When he answered the door, he found a young man with blood around his face. Harry helped the young man into his house and sat him in front of the fire. Before he could get the young man a drink of water, he was attacked from behind by two youths. Everything happened so quickly, he did not see enough of his attackers to give a clear description. Harry cried out for help as the intruders punched and kicked him.

Jenny lives across the road from Harry. She pulled the emergency cord to summon help from the warden. Mary, the warden, and her husband, Jeff, responded to Jenny's emergency call. When they arrived at Jenny's house, they saw three youths running away from Harry's home. As the complex is well lit they were able to see the three youths clearly. Jeff went into Harry's home and found him unconscious on the floor. Jeff called the police and ambulance to attend the scene. Harry's pension, which he had collected that day, was missing. Harry was taken to hospital where he was kept for four days for observation. His wounds needed eight stitches.

After a thorough police investigation, Mary and Jeff were able to identify the three young people. The young men aged fourteen, fifteen and sixteen were charged with robbery and occasioning grievous bodily harm. They pleaded not guilty to the charges and their case was referred to a youth court for consideration.

The charges

Robbery in the eyes of the law is stealing by using, or threatening to use, force. Mugging involves violence when stealing and is robbery in the eyes of the law. Bodily harm can be actual or grievous (more serious). Both are considered serious offences by the police.

Sentence for robbery

For a robbery the court could choose one of the following sentences for a person under the age of seventeen:

- community service – up to 120 hours if the offender is sixteen and up to 240 hours if the offender is seventeen or above. Offenders must be sixteen to do community service.

- probation – offenders must be seventeen to do probation, which can be set from six months to three years.

- a combination of probation and community service.

- curfew order – the offender is required to be indoors by a certain time at night for a set period.

- binding order – the offender promises never to offend again. If they do, they are punished for the old offence and the new one.

- supervision order – the offender has to be looked after and helped by a social worker or someone from a youth offending team for up to three years.

- attendance centre order – the offender has to attend a particular centre for a number of hours at particular times. Attendance can be set from 12 to 36 hours.

- fine – the amount will depend on the seriousness of the offence, the person's age, past behaviour and ability to pay. The maximum fine a youth court can impose is £1000.

- absolute discharge – the offender is not punished at all. This may be given if the person was charged with a minor offence or the circumstances leading to the offence were beyond the person's control.

- conditional discharge – this may be given if the offender undertakes not to re-offend during a set period of up to three years. If the person re-offends, then he or she can be punished for both offences.

Parents of 16–17 year olds who have been convicted may be told they must look after their children properly – if they fail to do so they can be fined up to £1000. If the children are under sixteen, a parenting order is used to make sure that parents control their children.

Failure to keep to a parenting order, which can include training for parents, will result in a fine of up to £1000.

Sentences for grievous bodily harm

For causing grievous bodily harm the court can give any of the sentences shown above or a custodial sentence. A youth court can give a custodial sentence of up to twelve months for two or more offences. Offenders can be kept for longer periods for first offences in very serious cases. If given a custodial sentence:

- 12–14 year olds will be taken to a secure training centre

- 15–20 year olds will be taken to a young offenders institution.

Activities

1 In groups of three you are to be the panel of magistrates considering Harry's case. What do you think the sentence should be and why?

2 'It's wrong to make someone suffer.' Talk about this statement in groups.

3 Write to the clerk at your local magistrates' court and ask what the different sentences are for shoplifting.

4 What do you think of people who attack the elderly for the price of their pensions? Talk about this in pairs.

Check it out

What you should have learned from this chapter

Look at the areas of study in the table. You should now know and understand the language and ideas that we have explored through Chapter 5: Criminal and civil law.

The activities and questions in the chapter, and the extra sheets your teacher will have worked through with you, should have helped you to learn about this topic.

If some of the areas are not clear, read through the pages again. If you are still not sure, ask your teacher to explain them again.

Area of study	Page
How does the law affect you?	79
Parents' duties	80
Consumers and the law	81
Young people and employment	83
The law and discrimination	83
What is crime?	85
Law-making in action	87
European laws	89
I'll see you in court! (criminal and civil law)	89
The rights of accused people	91
People in the legal system	91

You should be able to answer all the following questions. These are short answer questions similar to those that will appear in Section A of the written exam paper that you will sit at the end of the course.

The knowledge and ideas covered in this chapter will also be tested in longer, more detailed questions in Sections B and D of the exam paper.

1   At what age can you have a job?
2   How old do you have to be to have a passport of your own?
3   Name three Acts of Parliament which are involved with consumer law.
4   List three different types of discrimination.
5   Where are police records stored?
6   Explain the term 'reprimand'.
7   What is the difference between criminal and civil law?
8   List the stages of how a bill passes through Parliament and becomes a law.
9   What is the CPS?
10 What does a jury do?
11 Name three of the rights an accused person has.

6 The media

How much does the media influence our lives?

The media is one of the most persuasive influences on life in the modern world. The media includes:

- television
- radio
- videos
- magazines
- newspapers
- books
- the Internet
- advertisements
- the cinema.

These all play an important part in the life of many people in Western society.

In one form or another from an early age, the media influences our thoughts, our attitudes and, in some cases, our behaviour.

Freedom of speech

Article 19 of the United Nations Declaration of Human Rights states, 'Everyone has the right to freedom of opinions and expression'. This right allows you to hold your own opinions and to express your opinions in the media.

Censorship

In some countries the news services are controlled by the state. This gives the government a lot of power. It can stop people who do not share its views from reporting news. This is called censorship.

Propaganda

Propaganda is specially created information that aims to make people think in a certain way. Propaganda can be spread by many different media, although posters, leaflets, radio and the cinema are among the most widely used. Propaganda is often used in wartime.

Spin doctors

A spin doctor is someone who tries to control how the public thinks about a story by telling it in a certain way. The information is 'moved around' to make the reader or viewer look at one aspect. We say the story has been given 'a

Chinese propaganda poster (1966), showing Chairman Mao as the 'father of communism'

spin'. Most senior members of the government have spin doctors working for them. Spin doctors usually try to manipulate the media by:

- speaking to reporters off the record, i.e. without having their names mentioned in articles

- leaking information before a media story is released

- controlling the focus of attention in a news story

- choosing what news to release, when to release it and how to release it to the media.

Spin doctors control the amount of information given to the media at certain times. They can create a 'slow news' day when they want people to focus on a particular policy or document. When they want to 'hide' a story, they will present other issues to the media to create a 'fast news' day. Spin doctors also work for large companies, charities and pressure groups.

Who owns the media?

The mass media is the name given to the different ways information is given to a huge number of people. The mass media includes television, radio, newspapers and magazines, and the Internet. The way information is delivered to the public, for example a particular newspaper or television programme, is known as a media outlet. Individual people who own newspapers are known as press barons. Individual people who own media companies are known as media barons. An example is Rupert Murdoch, the head of News International which owns Sky Television, the *Sun*, *The Times* and other companies.

Rupert Murdoch – media baron

Fair reporting

The public relies on the media to provide up-to-date, non-biased information, so it is important that news is reported fairly.

Up-to-date and fairly reported information is also important because it gives us the information and views so we can form our own opinion.

So who controls the media?

Some people are worried that only a few people and companies control such a large number of the world's media outlets. Especially as only a small number of powerful individuals and international news services from the developed world control much of the media. Some people are worried that very few of these people come from less developed countries. Other people think that the media has ways of checking what it does and that it gives a fair view of the world.

There is a danger that the media will be biased towards a particular belief or value system. As media companies have grown, the media increasingly report news stories from all over the world. Some people argue that news stories are biased towards Western ideas and values. This is very clear in times of war, when the media tends to support the government and the nation's armed forces.

Monitoring the media

The operation of the media in the UK is monitored by two main bodies whose job is to control the standards of reporting information to the public. These bodies monitor television, advertising and press coverage of events.

The Press Complaints Commission (PCC) checks that the code of practice for publications is followed. This code has been used since 1991. The Code of Practice Committee is made up of editors from different newspapers and magazines. If a newspaper is found guilty of not keeping to the code, it must print what it did wrong in the newspaper. Among others, the code covers the following issues:

- Publications must not print inaccurate material.

- An opportunity for reply must be given to individuals or organizations.

- *Everyone is entitled to respect for their private life, home, health and correspondence.

- A person should not expect to be harassed or followed by journalists or photographers.

- *Children under sixteen should not be interviewed without an adult being present and without the agreement of their parents.

- *The names of children under the age of sixteen involved in sex cases must not be given.

- Journalists should not obtain or try to obtain information or pictures by deceiving people.

- The press must avoid being prejudiced, for example with regard to race, religion or disability.

- Journalists have a moral responsibility to protect people who speak to them in confidence.

- Payment for articles must be made openly and through an agent or with a witness.

There may be exceptions to the clauses marked * where publication can be shown to be in the public interest. The public interest includes:

- investigating and reporting on crime

- protecting public health and safety

- preventing the public from being misled by some statement or action of an individual or organization.

The PCC will require a full explanation in any case where publication is claimed to be in the public interest. In the case of a child the editor has to be very clear about the public interest. The PCC insists that children are protected.

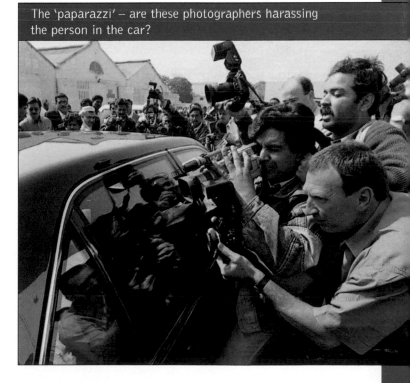

The 'paparazzi' – are these photographers harassing the person in the car?

Television

Television viewing has become the main leisure activity for many families and elderly people in Britain. On an average day 38 million people in Britain will turn on the television and watch it for three hours. This means that the average Briton will spend eight years watching 'the box'. It is said that television:

An Internet café in India

- tells us what we should think, what we should buy, what success is, what makes us happy, and how we should behave

- removes people from the world outside their living room

- has reduced children's ability to create imaginative games. This view is supported by evidence from teachers

- influences children – people report that television influences children more than school

- makes us think that everyone should have wealth, power, physical beauty and strength.

Television is a strong and powerful tool in society. It should reinforce the best ideals and values.

The Internet

The Internet is a powerful tool in the sending and receiving of information. It should be remembered that the Internet is largely used in the developed countries, as computers are too expensive in many countries across the world. Although they rarely own their own computer, some people in LEDCs are able to use Internet cafes.

Many people are concerned about how easy it is to get information from the Internet. There is a danger that some people may set up websites with false information or pornographic material. Some people think that the Internet should be censored to make people safe.

(A) Activities

1 Try to work out how many hours you have spent watching or reading the media in the last week. Think about how much you have watched television or videos, read books, magazines or newspapers, used the Internet, etc. With a partner, compare your answers.

2 Look at the section on 'Fair reporting' on pages 98–9. Why is it important that news is reported fairly?

Are we influenced by advertising?

Advertising can be heard on the radio and seen on television, at the cinema, on billboards, on public transport and in newspapers and magazines. We can even find advertisements on the clothes we wear!

Manufacturers spend large amounts of money to advertise their goods. Some radio and television companies get the money to make programmes from advertising.

Some people think that advertising makes people buy things that they don't really want or need. Other people believe that advertisements are a way of telling the general public about the range of products available to them.

Who checks on advertisements?

Television advertising is regulated by the Independent Television Commission. Radio advertising is regulated by the Radio Authority. These organizations are not controlled by the media companies or the government. An advertising code sets out the rules for advertising on radio and television.

Advertisements which do not take the rules into account may be banned. Advertisements which are meant for children 'must not include any material which might result in harm to them either physically, mentally or morally.'

(A) Activities

1 Find the names of five television programmes which are sponsored.

2 Choose any advertisement for an item of clothing. In a group, talk about who you think the advertisement is aimed at and whether it is successful.

3 Find two adverts that use personalities, for example footballers or pop stars, to encourage people to buy a product. What effect do you think this has on the public?

4 Prepare an advertisement for a product. Where would you want the advertisement to appear? Give reasons for your answer.

Famous 'faces' sell products with sponsorship

Comparative study: The media

Three main types of newspaper are on sale in Britain today – national, regional and local. National newspapers are sold across the country. Regional newspapers are sold over a large area. Local newspapers are sold in a small local area. National and local newspapers often cover different types of news. Similarly, national newspapers differ in the choice of news items they cover and the way in which they present the same event.

Newspapers use photographs and written reports to give the reader information. They use words carefully to add their chosen focus to a story. The people who write newspaper articles know that using emotional language can make people interested in a story.

What's in a headline?

A headline

- attracts the reader's attention
- sums up the story
- stirs the reader's feelings
- makes the reader want to find out the rest of the story.

The headline helps to sell the paper.

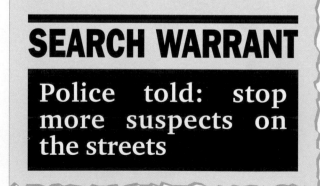

Figure 6.1 From the *Daily Mirror*, 11 March 2002.

The headline in Figure 6.1 is a play on the words 'search warrant'. We all recognize that a search warrant is the name of a legal document giving the police permission to search a property. Giving people warrant means giving permission. So the title is giving police permission to search people.

Using photographs and captions

Photographs are used to attract readers to buy the paper. Journalists try to make sure that they have a good photograph to back up their story. Captions are used to explain the meaning or the context of the photograph.

The photograph and caption below supported the headline in Figure 6.1. The article is about new powers for police in the stop and search procedure. If the caption is changed to 'Police criticized for use of force when searching', the focus of the article is changed.

POWERS: Police search a suspect

Facts and opinions

Every article printed in a newspaper will contain one or both of the following styles of writing:

- facts. A fact is something which can be proved to be true. News stories should answer the questions: Who? What? Where? When? Why?

- opinions. These are the views of the writer and are usually found on the letter pages, and in reviews and editorials. Sometimes it is difficult to tell opinion from fact. Sometimes opinions are written as if they are facts, for example:

  - Digital television is the greatest technological achievement of the twentieth century.
  - Robbie Williams is the best male singer ever.

Figure 6.2 is an editorial. While there are some facts in this editorial, it is based on the editor's opinion and feeling about the situation.

Comparing newspaper reports

The two newspaper reports in Figure 6.3 and 6.4 on pages 104 and 105 cover the same story – discussions which took place between British Prime Minister Tony Blair and other European leaders at the European Summit in Barcelona, Spain, during the weekend of 15–17 March 2002. One article appeared in the *Mirror* and the other in the *Guardian*. Both articles appeared on Saturday 16 March 2002.

You should read the two newspaper reports carefully at least twice. In order to compare the two articles you need to think about which aspects are the same and which are different. You should note down:

- facts that are in both articles (perhaps five)

- facts that are in one article but not in the other

- how the headline is used
- how the picture and caption are used, if appropriate.

VOICE OF THE Mirror

Don't play Saddam's mad game

SADDAM Hussein would be mad to take on the might of America. But of course that is exactly what he is.

He swaggeringly revels in once again becoming the focus of international debate.

He sees America preparing to launch an attack on Iraq and positively enjoys the prospect.

Like a bar-room brawler, he sneers at President Bush the equivalent of: 'Come on, big boy, let's see how tough you are.'

Saddam believes he cannot lose. He will either force the US to back down or suffer such terrible destruction of his country that Arab sympathy will be with him.

This is not a question of who is right and who is wrong. Saddam Hussein is an evil despot who crushes his own people and threatens the world.

But that does not mean an all-out military assault against him is the right way forward.

Mr Bush should listen to Jordan's King Abdullah. Yesterday he warned that an attack on Iraq would undermine the war on terrorism and destabilise the Middle East.

Saddam needs to be neutralised and controlled. Not made stronger.

Figure 6.2 From the *Daily Mirror*, 13 March 2002

BLOODY DANGEROUS

By JAMES HARDY

EU's fear on Iraq attack

EUROPE yesterday told Tony Blair that an all-out assault on Iraq could threaten world peace.

As riot police clashed with thousands of anti-globalisation protesters outside the EU summit, it was made clear to the PM that any strikes against Saddam Hussein must have the full backing of the United Nations.

And Germany said it would only help fight a war against Iraq if it was backed by a UN mandate.

Mr Blair has used the EU summit in Spain to try to rally support from the other 14 countries.

But the resounding message was that the US and Britain must not go it alone – and military action must be a last resort.

Foreign Secretary Jack Straw put a brave face on the rebuff, insisting: 'The whole world has made a decision that Iraq poses a very serious threat to the international community.'

He added that the US had already stressed any decisions had to be 'talked over carefully'.

German leader Gerhard Schroeder accused the UK of putting relations with the US before its place in Europe. Although German forces currently in Kuwait would 'help out' if needed, he said only UN backing would see him send troops to Iraq.

Throughout the debate in Barcelona, running battles between police and protesters raged outside. Bottles and stones were thrown by the rioters, many of whom wore masks.

Bins were set alight and blazing tyres thrown on a train line.

More than 8 500 police have been drafted in from across Spain.

Briton Guy Taylor said the officers provoked the riot. He said: 'Police hit out with batons.'

Figure 6.3 From the *Daily Mirror*, 16 March 2002

The *Mirror* headline

The headline is large and heavy and uses language to stir people's feelings. The word 'bloody' could have more than one meaning. This report was on page 2 of the paper. The headline could refer to a possible attack on Iraq. Equally, it could refer to the battle between police and protestors. The standfirst (the print below the headline which explains the main headline) indicates that the story is about the EU Summit, but the picture supports the story being about police and protestors.

Five facts in the *Mirror* article

- The message from the EU is that Britain and the US must not go it alone.
- Police clash with anti-globalization protestors.
- Description of 'riots' taking place.
- More than 8500 police officers have been drafted from across Spain.
- Fighter jets, anti-aircraft missiles and warships were on standby to counter (defend against) terrorist attacks.

Blair woos summit amid fears of split

Ian Black in Barcelona

There was mounting nervousness over the potential of the Iraq issue to cause divisions within the EU when Tony Blair canvassed the mood of his colleagues at the Barcelona summit last night.

Turkey, a key member of Nato, warned against any attack, arguing that Iraq did not constitute a threat to its neighbours. 'We feel that Iraq should not be the subject of military attacks because it would upset the whole Middle East,' the prime minister Bulent Ecevit told reporters after meeting EU leaders.

Mr Blair discussed the looming crisis with Gerhard Schröder, the German chancellor, but made clear that no decision had been made on specific measures to be taken against the Iraqi president. 'We are not at the stage of decisions,' the prime minister insisted.

Belgium, which this week proposed sending a high-level EU mission to Baghdad, was preparing a statement to be issued when the summit ends today.

Formally, the EU has no policy on Iraq because of sharp disagreements between Britain and France: but all 15 members are urging Baghdad to abide by UN security council disarmament resolutions.

Jack Straw, the foreign secretary, kept up the drumbeat, emphasising agreement on the threat so far and sidestepping evident divisions about the way ahead. 'The whole world has made a decision that Iraq poses a very serious threat to the security of the region and to the security of the international community,' he said.

It has not escaped the notice of his co-summiteers that Mr Blair was the only EU leader visited by US vice-president Dick Cheney this week.

EU members hope pressure on Saddam will oblige him to bow to demands that he readmit UN weapons inspectors.

'If there is military action it will not take place in 24 hours,' the EU's foreign policy chief, Javier Solana, told the BBC. 'We will have plenty of time. We want to see how the situation may evolve in New York and the United Nations.'

Figure 6.4 From *The Guardian*, 16 March 2002

The *Guardian* headline

The *Guardian* article was not trying to be emotional or dramatic, so the headline is a description of events. It uses words like 'woo' and 'fear' to attract the reader's interest.

Five facts in the *Guardian* article

- Turkey warned against attacking Iraq.

- EU stressed that Iraq should be urged to abide by UN Security Council disarmament resolutions (encouraged to get rid of its arms).

- Belgium suggested an EU mission to Baghdad.

- Mr Cheney, the US vice-president, visited Tony Blair this week.

- Quote from EU foreign policy spokesman that military action against Iraq is not about to begin.

Five common facts

- The discussions took place in Barcelona.

- Tony Blair talked to German leader Gerhard Schröder at the summit.

- Other EU states will not act without the agreement of the UN.

- Both quote British Foreign Secretary Jack Straw, though one quote has been edited.

- Any attack on Iraq could threaten world peace or cause EU division.

(A) Activities

1 In pairs, study the editorial in Figure 6.2. Do you think the editorial is trying to inform, shock, persuade or advise? Why do you think this?

2 Suggest two different headlines for the story about police stop-and search-powers (Figure 6.1) and two different captions for the photograph (page 102). Make notes of your suggestions.

Check it out

What you should have learned from this chapter

Look at the areas of study in the table. You should now know and understand the language and ideas that we have explored in Chapter 6: The media.

The activities and questions in the chapter, and the worksheets your teacher will have worked through with you, should have helped you to learn about this topic.

If some of the areas are not clear, read through the pages again. If you are still not sure ask your teacher to explain them again.

Area of study	Page
Freedom of speech	97
Who owns the media?	97
Fair reporting	98
Monitoring the media	99
Television	100
The Internet	100
Are we influenced by advertising?	101
Who checks on advertisements?	101

You should be able to answer all the following questions. These are short answer questions similar to those that will appear in Section A of the written exam paper that you will sit at the end of the course.

The knowledge and ideas covered in this chapter will also be tested in longer, more detailed questions in Sections B and D of the exam paper.

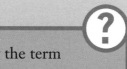

1. What do we mean by the term the media?
2. Name one media baron.
3. List four daily newspapers.
4. Name an international news company.
5. Which organization is responsible for monitoring publications?
6. Who monitors advertising?
7. What does the term freedom of speech mean?
8. Explain what is meant by censorship.
9. Name three effects that people say television has on our lives.

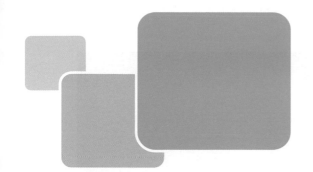

Global citizenship

Key ideas

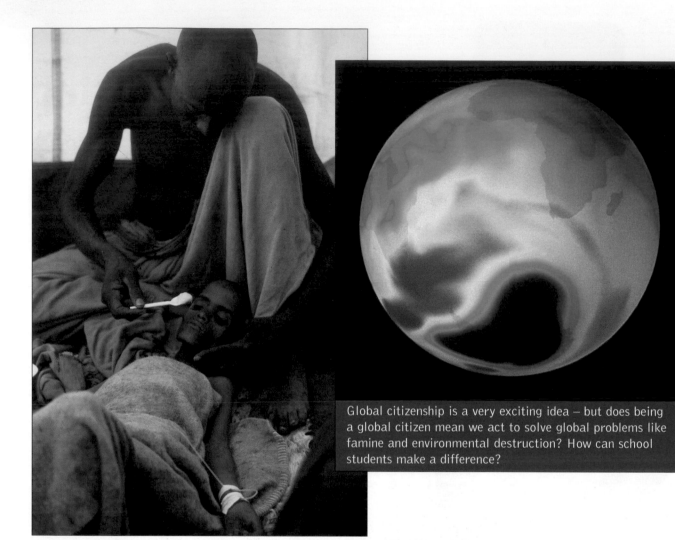

Global citizenship is a very exciting idea — but does being a global citizen mean we act to solve global problems like famine and environmental destruction? How can school students make a difference?

Can an unprovoked war on any country be justifiable? What can we do to make sure we communicate **without** using force?

7 International relations

The Commonwealth and the United Nations

In the past, each country controlled its own goods and services. This meant that the economy of one country was separate from the economy of another country. In recent years, the world economy has become more global. This is because trade has increased, companies are larger and communication is easier. As a result, countries have started to co-operate with each other. Groups of countries now work together to trade.

The UK's relationship with the Commonwealth and the UN

As a member of the EU, the Commonwealth and the UN, the UK often has to take care that it does not damage its relationships with one or other of these organizations. EU trading practices could conflict with long-standing trading agreements the UK has with Commonwealth countries. Similarly, the UK may be involved in a decision made by the Commonwealth countries which has not been agreed by the UN. The Foreign Office is in charge of the UK's relations with these organizations.

The Commonwealth

The countries which formed the British Empire are now linked together in an organization called the Commonwealth.

The Commonwealth conference

The Commonwealth was created in 1931. It is made up of 54 countries. Canada, Australia, New Zealand and the UK have been Commonwealth partners since 1931. Other countries joined at different times.

Heads of state from Commonwealth countries meet every two years for a conference. Every four years the athletes from Commonwealth countries compete in the Commonwealth Games. In 2002 these games were held in Manchester.

The Commonwealth supports free trade between member countries. Some people believe that this loose association of countries looks back to the time when Britain had an empire. Other people are proud of Britain's past and its relationship with this group of nations around the world today.

 Activities

1 From the Commonwealth website find out the aims of the Commonwealth.

2 Do you think the Commonwealth is a good idea? Talk about this in groups.

The aims of the United Nations

The United Nations (UN) was created after World War II. It aims to encourage international peace, security and co-operation. The UK was one of the original members. The United Nations Assembly is made up of representatives of each of the 185 member countries. Each country has one vote. Resolutions are discussed by the assembly. A UN resolution is respected in most countries of the world.

Each member country must give a minimum of 0.1 per cent of the UN budget. Payments are made in US dollars. It is difficult for some poorer countries to pay in dollars as their currencies do not have as much value as the dollar. Sometimes, powerful countries like the USA do not pay all that they should to the UN. This has led to some UN projects not taking place.

To be a member of the UN a country must sign the United Nations Charter. By signing this, member states agree to support the aims and objectives of the UN. These include:

- keeping international peace and security
- controlling arms
- protecting human rights
- giving aid to refugees and famine victims.

The UN has prepared guidelines and laws which set out how it carries out its aims and objectives.

The UN building in New York

How is the UN organized?

The UN is governed by a charter and has rules about how to carry out its work.

> *i*
>
> **The UN Secretariat** is based in New York and is headed by the Secretary-General of the United Nations. The Secretary-General is elected by the General Assembly and is responsible for running the UN.
>
> **The UN General Assembly** meets every year. It is made up of representatives of the 185 members of the UN. Developing countries outnumber developed countries by three to one on this council. A two-thirds majority is necessary for a decision to be made, so it is often difficult to reach an agreement.
>
> **The UN Security Council** was set up after World War II. The council has five permanent members – the UK, China, France, Russia and the USA – and ten temporary members. The five permanent members have the right to stop any decision. The Security Council's job is to discuss threats to international security, to suggest solutions or propose action. Action could include no longer trading with a country or stopping aid to a country. Military force is used as a last resort.

UN peacekeeping forces

One of the roles undertaken by the UK for the UN is that of peacekeeper (see photo, right). At times of conflict or disorder in a country the UN asks member states if they will provide defence troops from their armed forces to form a peacekeeping force in that country. The UK was involved in Afghanistan in two ways in 2002. The UK was fighting with the USA to remove terrorists from Afghanistan after the attack on the World Trade Center on 11 September 2001. At the same time, 2000 British troops were part of the 4800-strong international force which the UN placed in Afghanistan. The job of the international force was to support the new government and keep peace in the country.

Being part of a peacekeeping force is not without its cost. During a period of five years 60 members of the British armed forces lost their lives undertaking peacekeeping duties in the Balkans, Sierra Leone and Afghanistan.

A UN peacekeeping force in action

The UN Environment Programme (UNEP)

The UNEP was set up to review the global environment. It is responsible to the UN for protecting the global environment for future generations. The UNEP is based in Nairobi, Kenya. The UNEP has the power to name protected species of animals and plants and to create protected areas for them.

In addition, this programme deals with research into the effect global warming and acid rain will have on the environment. A UN Conference on Environment and Development was held in Rio de Janeiro in 1992. At the conference countries agreed to implement UNEP Agenda 21 – a plan of action to improve the environment which should be put in place locally, nationally and globally.

Another conference was held in Kyoto, Japan, in 1997. This conference showed that many of the Agenda 21 plans had not been started. The conference reports show that the UN cannot force member countries to act upon the decisions made at the UN or any of its conferences.

UN Commission on Human Rights

The UN Universal Declaration of Human Rights led to the creation of a UN commission to monitor its operation. The commission monitors human rights abuses such as torture or discrimination. It reports human rights abuses to the UN General Assembly. It is helped in its work by non-governmental organizations (NGOs) such as Amnesty International.

The UN Conference at Rio (1992)

A Activities

1 Should the UN have more power to make governments keep to environmental targets? Talk about this in groups.

2 From the UN website find out what Article 2 of the UN Declaration of Human Rights says. Why is it important?

3 Look at the Amnesty International website. Find information about one of their human rights campaigns. You could find out:

- where the campaign is taking place
- what human rights abuse it is trying to fight
- how it is trying to make changes
- how individuals have helped with the campaign
- what the results of the campaign have been so far.

i The nineteen member countries of NATO are:

Belgium	UK
Canada	USA
Denmark	Germany
France	Greece
Iceland	Spain
Italy	Turkey
Luxembourg	Czech Republic
Netherlands	Hungary
Norway	Poland
Portugal	

Flags of the countries in the UN

The UK and NATO

The North Atlantic Treaty was signed in Washington on 4 April 1949. This created the North Atlantic Treaty Organization (NATO), an alliance of twelve independent countries including the UK. Four further European countries joined the organization between 1952 and 1982. On 12 March 1999 the Czech Republic, Hungary and Poland joined the alliance to bring the total number of members to nineteen.

NATO created:

- the North Atlantic Co-operation Council in 1991
- the Partnership for Peace in 1994
- the Euro-Atlantic Partnership Council in 1997.

These agreements set up new forms of partnership in the Mediterranean and Eastern Europe. In 1997 NATO agreed on future relations with Russia.

The main purpose of NATO is to protect the freedom and security of its member countries. Its first task is to defend any member country.

NATO forces on exercise in Kosovo

To do this, NATO tries to prevent one country attacking another and takes action to resolve any crisis. NATO is committed to working with other countries in the Euro-Atlantic area. It aims to increase trust among its members and the capacity for joint action. As part of this co-operation, NATO led a multinational force in Bosnia to help build the basis for future peace in the region. Similarly, it leads a multinational force in Kosovo (see the photo above), aimed at reversing the ethnic tension in the country so thousands of Kosovan refugees can return safely to their homeland.

For fifty years NATO has tried to improve co-operation between countries. Member countries meet regularly to discuss issues of joint interest and concern and to plan future areas of co-operation. The armed forces of the member countries, including those of the UK, join together to undertake planned military exercises. This builds trust, confidence and understanding so these separate military units can work together if a conflict arises.

 Activities

1   Look at the map of the EU on page 75 and the list of NATO countries on page 113. Which members of NATO are members of the EU?

2   Look at the photo above of NATO forces in Kosovo. Use the Internet to answer the following questions:
   • Why did NATO send a peacekeeping force to Kosovo?
   • What is the peacekeeping force doing?
   • How long do you think this operation might take?

Case study: International conflict – Iraq

Events leading to the Gulf War

Iraq was in debt after its war with Iran which ended in 1988. Iraq owed £70 billion, half of which was owed to the Gulf states, mainly Kuwait (Figure 7.1). Saddam Hussein, President of Iraq, said that members of the Arab League were waging 'economic war' on Iraq by keeping oil prices low. The Iraqis accused Kuwait of stealing Iraq's oil.

Towards the end of July, the world was faced with a Middle East crisis when 30 000 Iraqi troops moved to the Kuwaiti border. US Ambassador to Iraq, April Glaspie, warned Iraq that the USA would use its powers to protect its friends in the Gulf. On 27 July, Kuwait agreed to Iraq's demands for compensation, but refused to give up the islands of Bubiyan and Warba to Iraq. By this time, Iraq had 100 000 troops on the Kuwaiti border. It took only one day for Iraq to take over Kuwait. This happened on 2 August 1990.

The UN Security Council was called to an emergency session and an emergency meeting of Arab League foreign ministers was held in Cairo. The UN imposed economic sanctions which meant that other countries stopped trading with Iraq. The UN set a deadline of 15 January 1991 for Iraq to withdraw from Kuwait.

As the deadline approached, UN-controlled forces began to collect in the Gulf area. The force included naval ships, air attack equipment, tanks and other armoured fighting vehicles. Warships came from Australia, Britain, Canada, Holland, France, Italy and the USA. Despite warnings from the UN and governments across the world, Iraq did not withdraw. On Wednesday 16 January 1991, the war began.

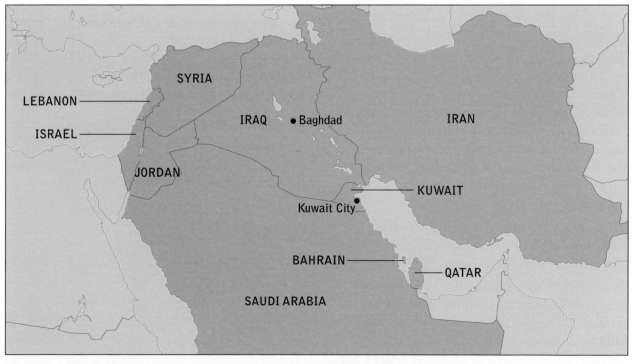

Figure 7.1 The Gulf region

US soldiers in the Gulf War

UN Resolutions

Resolution 660 – 2 August 1990

- Condemned invasion of Kuwait
- Demanded Iraq's withdrawal

Resolution 661 – 6 August 1990

- Stopped Iraq and occupied Kuwait from trading with other countries
- Set up a special committee to make sure resolution was followed
- Called upon UN members to protect property of Kuwait around the world

Resolution 687 – 3 April 1991

- Formally ended Gulf War
- Arranged the inspection of Iraq's suspected weapons of mass destruction

Resolution 986 – 14 April 1995

- Approved sale of Iraqi oil in exchange for food and other aid

Resolution 1115 – 21 June 1997
Resolution 1134 – 23 October 1997

- Demanded that Iraq allow weapon inspections

Resolution 1137 – 12 November 1997

- Stopped senior Iraqi officials from travelling abroad

The Gulf War

The Gulf War, Operation Desert Storm, lasted 44 days from 16 January until 28 February 1991. During this time allied forces, including the USA and Britain, fought to make sure UN resolutions were followed. The allied forces were led by American General Norman Schwarzkopf.

Troops came from many countries in the world including the USA, Britain, France, Canada and Australia. Other countries allowed the allied forces to use their facilities, for example airports were used for refuelling and docks for restocking ships. Countries in the EU and across the world gave money to support the allied effort to drive Iraq from Kuwait.

Fighting in the air lasted for forty days. Fighting on the ground started on day 40 and Kuwait City was set free on day 42.

It is difficult to establish the number of people killed in this conflict. The Iraqis tended to exaggerate the number of people killed and injured, while the allies tried to minimize the numbers. Those who died were only part of the human cost of the war to the people of Iraq.

Continuing conflict

Since the end of the Gulf War in 1991, the conflict has continued between the USA and Iraq. Several times violence has broken out (see Figure 7.3 on page 118). Tension between the USA and Iraq started to build up again after the bombing of the World Trade Center in New York on 11 September 2001.

The causes

The main cause of the continued conflict between the USA and Iraq is disagreement over the need for UN inspections. The US and the UN claim that Iraq is not keeping to the agreement made at the end of the Gulf War as it is continuing to develop weapons of mass destruction. Iraq denies these claims and says that the USA is trying to cripple the country through continued economic sanctions.

Another point of disagreement is the 'no-fly zones' (see Figure 7.2) over northern and southern Iraq. These were originally designed to protect the Kurdish minority in the north and the Shiite minority in the south. These zones are Iraqi airspace in which Iraqi planes are not allowed to fly.

The wreckage in Kuwait after the Gulf War

Iraq says that it is being punished unfairly by the USA. The USA says that Saddam Hussein and his government are responsible for the continuing action against Iraq because Iraq has not kept to the UN resolutions.

After the attacks in New York in September 2001, George W Bush, the American President, stated that every effort would be made to remove the terrorists and that the countries who helped them, including Iraq, would be punished.

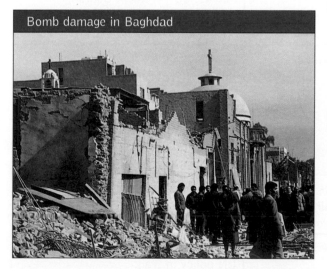
Bomb damage in Baghdad

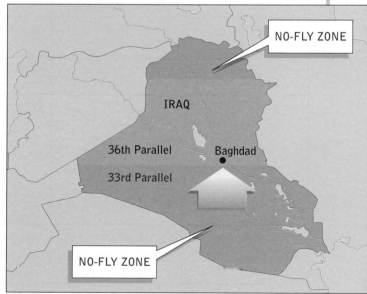

Figure 7.2 Map of 'no-fly zones' in Iraq (1992 Magellan Geographix, Santa Barbara, CA)

Date	Countries involved	Type of action	Details of action
2 August 1992	USA and UN vs Iraq	Establishment of 'no-fly' zone	No-fly zone created over south Iraq. USA begins air patrols of the zone.
28 December 1992	USA vs Iraq	Air fighting to stop planes entering 'no-fly' zone	US plane shoots down Iraqi Mig-25 when it enters the 'no-fly' zone.
13 January 1993	USA, UK and France vs Iraq	Air and missile strike	Gulf forces strike Iraqi radar and missile sites.
17 January 1993	USA vs Iraq	Missile strike	USA strike nuclear facility outside Baghdad to punish Iraq for not allowing UN weapons inspections.
27 June 1993	USA vs Iraq	Missile strike	USA fires 24 missiles from ships at military headquarters in Baghdad to stop plot to kill former President Bush.
7 October 1994	USA and Kuwait vs Iraq	Military build-up to a new crisis	US planes and 54 000 troops head for the Gulf as Iraq's troops prepare to attack Kuwait. Iraq pulls back its army.
31 August 1996	Iraq and KDP (Kurdistan Democratic Party) vs PUK (Patriotic Union of Kurdistan)	Iraq helps one group in Kurdish civil war	Iraq seizes city of Irbil inside the Kurdish 'protected area' in northern Iraq, which is protected by US-led troops.
3–4 September 1996	USA vs Iraq	Missile strikes	USA fires missiles at Iraqi military targets. US President Clinton extends 'no-fly' zones to cover parts of Baghdad and central Iraq.
16–20 December 1998	USA and UK vs Iraq	Missile strikes	Operation Desert Fox – attacks on sites relating to production of nuclear, chemical and biological weapons because Iraq failed to co-operate with UN inspections. As a result, Iraq says it would end all inspections and not accept the 'no-fly' zones.
29–30 December 1998	USA and UK vs Iraq	Iraq fires missiles on US aircraft in 'no-fly' zone	Allied forces respond and destroy Iraqi defences.
December 1998 –present	USA and UK vs Iraq	Continued missile attacks	Allied forces continue to support UN policy in Iraq.

Figure 7.3 Iraq – the continuing conflict

The effects of sanctions

UNICEF and other UN organizations agree that the sanctions have been terrible for the people of Iraq (Figures 7.4 and 7.5). It is estimated that up to 1 million people have died from starvation and disease in the last ten years. Some people would argue that sanctions have strengthened Saddam Hussein's position in Iraq.

Saddam Hussein among his followers

Christian Aid's experience of sanctions

The immediate consequence of eight years of sanctions has been a dramatic fall in living standards, the collapse of the infrastructure, and a serious decline in the availability of public services. The long-term damage to the fabric of society has yet to be assessed but economic disruption has already led to heightened levels of crime, corruption and violence.

Figure 7.4 From *Working in Iraq: Christian Aid's Experience 1990–1998*, Christian Aid

Squeezed to death

The change in 10 years is unparalleled in my experience. In 1989, the literacy rate was 95%; and 93% of the population had free access to modern health facilities. Parents were fined for failing to send their children to school. The phenomenon of children begging was unheard of. Iraq had reached a stage where the basic indicators we use to measure the overall well-being of human beings, including children, were some of the best in the world. Now it is in the bottom 20%. **In 10 years, child mortality has gone from one of the lowest in the world to one of the highest.**

Figure 7.5 John Pilger quotes UNICEF's senior representative in Iraq, Anapama Rao Singh, from *The Guardian*, 4 March 2000

(A) Activities

1 Look at the photos on pages 116 and 117 carefully. Choose one photo and describe it in detail.

2 Are the UN and the US right to continue with sanctions in Iraq? Talk about this in groups.

3 What do you think needs to be done to resolve this conflict? Talk about this in pairs.

Check it out

What you should have learned from this chapter

Look at the areas of study in the table. You should now know and understand the language and ideas that we have explored in Chapter 7: International relations.

The activities and questions in the chapter, and the worksheets your teacher will have worked through with you, should have helped you to learn about this topic.

If some of the areas are not clear, read through the pages again. If you are still not sure ask your teacher to explain them again.

Area of study	Page
What is the Commonwealth?	109
The aims of the United Nations	110
How is the UN organized?	111
UN peacekeeping forces	111
The UN Environment Programme	112
UN Commission on Human Rights	112
The role of NATO	113

You should be able to answer all the following questions. These are short answer questions similar to those that will appear in Section A of the written exam paper that you will sit at the end of the course.

The knowledge and ideas covered in this chapter will also be tested in longer, more detailed questions in Sections B and D of the exam paper.

1   What is the Commonwealth? When was the Commonwealth created?

2   How many countries belong to the Commonwealth?

3   What does UN stand for?

4   When was the UN created? How many countries belong to it?

5   Briefly explain what the Security Council does and who its members are.

6   Name three countries in which UN peacekeeping forces have operated.

7   Give an example of a project carried out by the UNEP.

8   What is the role of the UN Commission on Human Rights?

9   Name five members of NATO?

10   What is the main role of NATO?

8 World trade and overseas aid

Global inequality

The development gap

Figure 8.1 shows the way wealth was spread across the world in 1981 when the Brandt Commission reported its findings. In simple terms, the world is divided into two halves – the wealthy North and the poorer South. The main finding of this report was that two-thirds of the world's people lived in poverty while the remaining third enjoyed a large proportion of the world's wealth. This is known as the 'development gap'.

The United Nations now sorts the world's 206 nations into 'high income', 'middle income' and 'low income' countries. The 'high income' countries include the USA, Canada, Australia, Japan and most of Western Europe. These countries hold a particularly large share of the world's wealth. The 'middle income' countries include much of Latin America, the Middle East, Eastern Europe and individual countries in north and south Africa. The 'low income' countries mostly lie south of the equator. Their citizens live in poor conditions and many die from disease or hunger.

Developed countries

The most powerful countries in the world are those which are rich through having a developed economy. These countries are in Western Europe and North America. They have become known as the West. These countries have:

- low death rates
- low birth rates
- high life expectancy
- good communications
- good transport systems

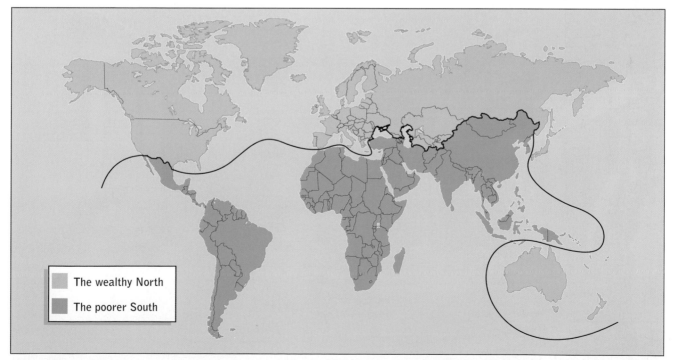

Figure 8.1 The North–South divide as shown by the Brandt Commission in 1981

- good public health and hygiene systems
- organized industry.

They are also known as More Economically Developed Countries (MEDCs).

Developing countries

Countries which are not yet fully industrialized are known as developing countries. These countries are often described as Third World countries.

These countries have:

- high death rates
- high birth rates
- low life expectancy
- poor transport systems
- poor communication
- poor public health and hygiene systems
- little organized industry.

Countries in the Third World have built up large debts which they are finding difficult to repay. The countries which still require major developments are known as Less Economically Developed Countries (LEDCs).

History will show that the Third World countries have not always been poor. Changes took place when European settlers from countries including Britain, France and Spain took over land overseas. They wanted to increase their economic and political power. The countries they took over were called colonies. The settlers took valuable resources from the countries and millions of young men and women were taken as slaves. Most African states are still dependent upon European countries for trade and finance.

The poverty gap between rich and poor widens

Who holds power?

People and organizations that have power can make individuals, groups of individuals or whole countries do what they want them to do. Sometimes coercion is used, which means making people do something they don't want to do. To study citizenship, you need to understand the types of power and their uses (see Figure 8.2).

Activities

1 Make a list of the differences between developing and developed countries.

2 Look at Figure 8.2. List the four types of power and give examples of organizations or countries that have each type of power.

Closing the development gap

Closing the development gap will not happen quickly, nor will it be easy. The export of raw materials is often the only source of income in a developing country. The raw materials are sold cheaply and the economy of the country is dependent on that income. Multinational companies have used this situation to their own advantage. They have set up factories in developing countries to take advantage of cheap labour, relaxed pollution laws and created new marketing opportunities.

Several attempts have been made to close the development gap, mainly through aid packages and investment programmes. Investment programmes will only work in a stable, peaceful country. The political problems in some developing countries, which can result in war, do not help economic development.

Political power allows governments to make laws, and make and enforce decisions. The United Nations usually has world political power.

Economic power means having the resources to buy, sell or produce goods and services. Large companies and corporations have economic power.

Social power is used to influence people's ideas and beliefs, and to organize and control large groups of people. Traditionally, religious organizations have had this type of power. With the growth of technology, the media now also has a great deal of social power.

Types of power

Military power could be seen as the ability to defend a country. It can also be seen as one country's ability to attack another country. Powerful countries, such as the USA and Russia, have large numbers of weapons including nuclear warheads.

Figure 8.2 Types of power

Trading practices

The World Trade Organization

Trade is the movement of goods and services between different countries. Most countries rely on trade to bring money into the country. Trade agreements control the import and export of goods between countries. The World Trade Organization is a UN agency. It meets to discuss issues relating to trade and the operation of agreements. It can also try to settle disputes. Many people believe that the free trade agreements in force are unfair on LEDCs. They think that fair trade agreements are needed which give workers a better deal.

Free trade versus Fairtrade

Many countries belong to free trade groups. The main aim of these trading groups is to encourage trade between particular countries. One of the largest trading groups is the EU. Oxfam sells products from Fairtrade organizations in its shops.

Free trade uses the raw materials of the LEDCs which have to export them at low prices. This has encouraged multinational manufacturers to set up in developing countries. As a result small local businesses and co-operatives have suffered.

Fairtrade agreements aim to give people in LEDCs the chance to benefit from trade and investment. Fairtrade organizations want to improve the working conditions of people and increase the amount of profit given to the workers.

Fairtrade, improving working conditions

The impact of multinational companies

Giant multinational companies are increasingly influential in the world's economy. These multinational companies are operated by a small number of people. They have developed steadily over many years within the market economy and firmly believe in free trade. The largest can match, or exceed, the size and scale of some countries in wealth, power and trading.

Multinational companies have grown in two ways:

- By natural growth – through the production of goods that sell well. The profits from these goods are put back into the company so it can develop and produce new consumer goods.

- By merger – through mergers with other companies producing similar services and goods.

As a result of mergers, multinational companies have moved their operations to various countries in the world, including LEDCs, where they can increase their production and profit. Multinational companies look for good transport networks and cheap labour when choosing a country to move to.

The development of communication technology has further helped the growth of

Multinationals are the new global culture

multinationals. Communication around the world is now easy and speedy. A decision made in New York can be in operation in India in minutes.

Multinational companies can also encourage LEDCs to develop their own industries. Taiwan is an example of a newly industrialized country (NIC). It now has twelve multinational companies.

(A) Activities

1. What is the purpose of fair trade agreements? Talk about how they can help LEDCs.

2. Look at the points below that describe some of the effects of multinational companies. Rewrite the points in two lists. The first list should include points that help the multinationals. The second should include points that help LEDCs. Multinationals:
   - believe in free trade
   - are very wealthy and powerful
   - give employment to local people
   - put profits back into the company to produce new goods
   - use cheap labour
   - encourage LEDCs to develop their own industries
   - make a large profit for the company.

Using your lists, talk about whether you think multinationals are good for the development of LEDCs.

Aid

Aid is the transfer of money, goods and skills from one country (the donor) to another (the recipient). Aid is usually given freely, but sometimes conditions are attached to the goods and services provided. For example, money might be given for ten projects to set up water pumps within a year. If the projects are not completed on time, some of the money might have to be given back. Aid falls into three categories.

Bilateral and multilateral aid

Bilateral aid is usually given by the government of one country to another as a low interest loan for a specific project. Bilateral aid is given by the UK and France to their former colonies.

Multilateral aid is the money given by governments to international agencies. The agencies decide how the money will be spent. Many of these agencies work under the UN.

Voluntary aid

Voluntary aid is given by non-government organizations (NGOs). These organizations are mainly charities such as Oxfam, Christian Aid and Save the Children. Most of the charities are based in industrialized countries. They raise money through public appeals, regular voluntary donations, mail order and charity shops. This aid is given for particular local needs and is usually very effective.

Relief aid is a short-term measure which deals with emergency situations. It is usually given in response to a natural disaster such as a flood, drought or earthquake. Food, medical help, clothing and blankets are supplied to give relief to survivors.

Development aid

Development aid is given by governments or NGOs as a long-term solution. It aims to increase a country's level of development by improving the quality of life of its people. It is used to improve health care, provide practical help for farmers, and develop local co-operatives and community projects. More and more aid agencies would like to concentrate on development aid as it helps people in LEDCs to provide everything they need to live.

Development aid is all about self-help, not charity

UN aid agencies

Aid is an important part of the work of the UN. It gives relief aid to countries from its funds. It also distributes the funding given by individual countries to cope with emergency situations.

Developmental aid, which is intended for longer-term projects such as providing clean water, is usually supported by NGOs, for example Oxfam or Christian Aid. The following are examples of UN aid agencies:

- The World Health Organization (WHO) aims to improve the health of the world's people. It tries to wipe out some of the many diseases which attack the developing world. In recent times, the WHO has tried to encourage healthy living. This includes advice on the best food to eat and support for people with mental health problems. It also deals with the UN's work to prevent diseases such as AIDS and help those who have the disease.

- The UN Development Programme (UNDP) is usually involved in activities in developing countries. A country may choose to improve its systems of education, transport, communications or healthcare. The UNDP would fund these projects.

- The World Food Programme provides food aid. Based in Rome, its aim is to get rid of world hunger. The programme deals with emergency relief aid in times of natural disaster.

- The UN Fund for Population Activities was established to help countries which need to control population growth. It helps with education and training as well as family planning.

(A) Activity

Put together information to provide a case study of the aid organization WaterAid. Visit www.heinemann.co.uk/hotlinks to find the following information:
- how WaterAid raises money
- what kind of aid it gives
- which countries or parts of the world it helps
- details of one of its aid programmes.

The World Food Programme distributing food

Sustainable development

What is sustainable development?

Sustainable development means that we should treat the world in a way that makes sure everyone has a better quality of life, now and in the future.

The 1992 Rio Summit

In 1992 the first United Nations Earth Summit was held in Rio de Janeiro, Brazil. This summit promised to tackle the main threats to our existence – poverty, hunger, war and environmental damage. Agenda 21 was one of the most important agreements made at the summit. Agenda 21 is a plan for moving towards sustainable development in the twenty-first century. More than 178 governments adopted the agenda.

Agenda 21 is based on the slogan, 'Think globally, act locally'. It sets out how to make development socially, economically and environmentally sustainable. Governments, regions, local councils, businesses, industry, local communities and individuals are expected to play their part in carrying out the aims of Local Agenda 21.

Outcomes of the Rio Summit

After the summit in Rio de Janeiro many people were keen to take action. But in some countries little was done. In the UK, local councils have adopted Agenda 21 policies for sustainable development. Despite this activity in the UK, many people believe that there is little sign of improvement.

Agriculture
Atmosphere
Biodiversity
Biotechnology
Capacity-building
Consumption and production patterns
Demographics
Desertification and drought
Education and awareness
Energy
Finance
Forests
Freshwater
Health
Human settlements
Indicators
Industry
Information
Integrated decisions
International law
Institutional matters
Land management
Major groups
Mountains
Oceans and seas
Poverty
Science
Small islands
Sustainable tourism
Technology
Toxic chemicals
Trade and environment
Transport
Waste (hazardous)
Waste (radioactive)
Waste (solid)

Figure 8.3 Agenda 21 issues

President George Bush, USA – key opponent of the Kyoto Protocol

The Kyoto Protocol

The third conference on climate change took place in December 1997 in Kyoto, Japan. Over 160 countries took part including all European nations. The conference adopted the Kyoto Protocol which agreed the following:

- MEDCs to cut greenhouse emissions by 5 per cent by 2012

- LEDCs to continue to cut carbon levels to 1990 levels by 2005.

MEDCs could reach these targets by

- introducing ways of saving more energy in industry

- introducing stricter standards in cars and electrical goods

- increasing activities to protect the environment such as recycling.

The USA has not accepted the Kyoto Protocol.

One of the main stumbling blocks to the success of the Rio Summit was the response of the USA. The USA did not like all aspects of the agreements and refused to sign them all. As a result many people complained that the USA hindered the negotiations at Rio. The USA believes that plans to protect the environment might interfere with the workings of the free market or slow down economic growth. Many people believe that no agreement or solution will work without US support.

A local recycling area

Local authority responses

To meet the aims of Local Agenda 21, local authorities around the world were requested to:

- start talking to citizens, local organizations and private companies
- adopt a local Agenda 21
- reach agreement with all groups in the local community
- create the best plans for development
- make sure people living in the area know about sustainable development and how they can help
- look at and make changes to existing programmes in line with Agenda 21 aims.

At a local level, councils would be required to make plans to:

- save energy and make sure air quality is good
- buy environmentally friendly goods and services and manage waste
- keep the variety of plants and animals in the local area and allow people to use the countryside
- encourage people to travel on foot, by bicycle or on public transport to cut air pollution

- consider the environment when making decisions on how to use land.

Every local authority in the UK was required to talk to local people and create an action plan. The plan had to set out what local authorities think are the most important actions to take in their area. It also had to include how and when they will take these actions.

Achieving sustainable development

To achieve sustainable development we need individuals, communities and businesses to change their way of life. We are using the world's resources at a greater rate than they can be replaced. We must learn not to pollute the air, water and soil. We must create less waste and stop harming the environment. Many of these changes can be made by individuals, but large industries and organizations must change their policies and play their part too. Otherwise the world's resources will run out.

People across the UK in local organizations and schools are getting involved with projects in their local community. Projects are arranged by groups such as the environmental charity BTCV (British Trust for Conservation Volunteers).

 Activities

1 Contact your local council and ask for its Agenda 21 information. Make notes on what your area plans to do.

2 Make a list of five things you could do to be more environmentally friendly. Talk about this with a partner.

3 Do you think that sustainable development is achievable? Talk about this in groups.

4 Visit the website for BCTV www.heinemann.co.uk/hotlinks to see what projects are in action now. Can you join in one of their projects?

Case study: Greenpeace – international agents of change

About Greenpeace

Greenpeace is an international organization with 2.5 million supporters in 158 countries. It relies on individual membership and support to fund its campaigns to protect the environment. Greenpeace was founded in 1971 when a group of people set out in a boat to protest about nuclear weapons testing off Canada. Today, Greenpeace has five ships that can go anywhere in the world.

Greenpeace communicates with over 6000 businesses and governments to persuade them that changes are necessary to make sure the environment is cleaner. Greenpeace is concerned with a wide range of environmental causes. Perhaps it is best known for its campaign to stop commercial whaling.

Non-violent direct action

Greenpeace believes in non-violent direct action. This is designed to:

- inform people about an issue
- put pressure on people in authority to change things
- protest at unfair treatment of some people
- change the situation.

The Indian pacifist leader Mahatma Ghandi said, 'In non-violence the masses have a weapon which enables a child, a woman, or even a decrepit old man to resist the mightiest government successfully'. Martin Luther King was a black civil-rights leader in the USA. He believed that the only way to achieve equality and change society's views was by non-violent and peaceful forms of protest. He explained the Non-Violent Creed as:

To resist without bitterness
To be cursed and not reply
To be beaten and not hit back.

The first Greenpeace ship – the *Phyllis Cormack*

Greenpeace with the whales

Greenpeace launched its anti-whaling campaign in 1975, when populations of the great whales had fallen to crisis levels. Most whales had been killed by a whaling industry that knew no bounds. Some species were almost extinct.

Using high-profile, non-violent direct actions at sea, public appeals and political lobbying, Greenpeace played a big part in stopping commercial whaling. This took effect in 1986, together with an international trade ban on whale products.

Nine countries were whaling when the agreement to stop took effect and seven ended their activities by 1990. Japan and Norway continued to hunt whales commercially. Today, these countries are pushing to lift the ban on whaling. This would have a devastating impact on the world's remaining whales.

The Greenpeace campaign is part of an international effort to communicate a simple but urgent message:

The time has come to protect whales permanently and end commercial whaling forever.

We are leading the global struggle through:
1 taking non-violent direct action against whalers
2 telling the world the truth about whaling
3 working with the regional whale watching industry to encourage whale watching instead of whaling
4 public education in countries around the world, including Japan and Norway
5 political lobbying in countries that have influence at the IWC (International Whaling Commission) and the CITES (Convention on the International Trade in Endangered Species)
6 taking part in annual meetings of the IWC and CITES.

Greenpeace intends to continue this effort until the world's whale populations are protected, permanently, from commercial whaling.

Figure 8.4 Adapted from the Greenpeace website. To visit their website go to www.heinemann.co.uk/hotlinks and insert express code 8176P.

Figure 8.5 Adapted from the Greenpeace membership leaflet

Five recent Greenpeace successes

1999 After ten years of campaigning, food manufacturers and UK supermarkets remove genetically modified ingredients from their products.

1999 Greenpeace launches its campaign to halt illegal logging in the Amazon rainforest.

2000 The British government finally rejects fridges that are harmful to the environment and accepts the advantages of greenfreeze technology.

2001 Greenpeace action closes the Sheffield incinerator and stops it giving off harmful poisonous gases and ash. This is part of the global campaign to manage waste in a way that does not harm the environment.

2001 Greenpeace and Power launch 'Juice' – a clean electricity product at no extra cost. It will supply 50 000 homes and encourage the development of a specific windfarm out at sea.

Tokyo stirs frenzy for whalemeat

From Robert Whymant in Tokyo

JAPAN is using ice-cream and musicals to win hearts and stomachs in its battle to lift the ban on commercial whaling at a critical International Whaling Commission (IWC) meeting in May.

Loudspeaker vans are touring the nation urging people to eat whalemeat and back the abolition of a 16-year-old moratorium on whale hunting. . . .

Motoji Nagasawa, who heads Greenpeace Japan's anti-whaling campaign, said: 'The government's strategy is to . . . make it appear whalemeat is important to the Japanese diet – the reverse of the truth.'

As in previous years, Japan plans to seek the resumption of coastal whaling when the IWC meets in Shimonoseki, western Japan . . .. The clash with anti-whaling countries such as the United States and Britain is expected to be particularly fierce this year, because Japan says that it intends to step up 'scientific' killing of whales, including an endangered species.

In 1986 Tokyo complied reluctantly with the ban on commercial whaling, but quickly began bringing in carcasses disguised as 'scientific research whaling'. Last year Japanese whalers brought home 440 from Antarctica, and 158 from the northwest Pacific, for sale to restaurants after perfunctory tests to determine diet and migration patterns.

Millions of pounds are being spent to mask an embarrassing fact: that a majority of Japanese would prefer whale-watching to whale-eating.

'It's a complete deception. Nobody in today's Japan considers whalemeat important to our diet,' Mr Nagasawa said. 'There's none in my supermarket. And there's no vital economic interest. Only about 300 people work full-time in whaling.'

A recent government survey said that about 70 per cent of Japanese back a resumption of whaling, and nearly 90 per cent had eaten whalemeat at least once. The findings were at odds with a survey conducted by MORI with a Japanese partner two years ago on behalf of Greenpeace.

Figure 8.6 Adapted from *The Times*, 23 March 2002

Activities

1 Japan continues to whale for 'scientific' reasons. Japan caught 598 whales in 2001. Should this be allowed? Talk about this in groups.

2 Use the Greenpeace website to list five current Greenpeace campaigns.

3 Whaling and eating whale meat has been a part of culture in countries like Japan for many years. Why should this have to change? Talk about this in groups.

Check it out

What you should have learned from this chapter

Look at the areas of study in the table. You should now know and understand the language and ideas that we have explored in Chapter 8: World trade and overseas aid.

The activities and questions in the chapter, and the worksheets your teacher will have worked through with you, should have helped you to learn about this topic.

If some of the areas are not clear, read through the pages again. If you are still not sure ask your teacher to explain them again.

You should be able to answer all the following questions. These are short answer questions similar to those that will appear in Section A of the written exam paper that you will sit at the end of the course.

The knowledge and ideas covered in this chapter will also be tested in longer, more detailed questions in Sections B and D of the exam paper.

Area of study	Page
The development gap	121
Who holds power?	123
The World Trade Organization	124
Free trade versus Fairtrade	124
Multinational companies	125
Aid programmes	126
Agenda 21 and sustainable development	128
Local responses to Agenda 21	130

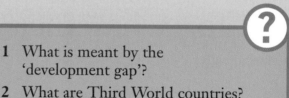

1 What is meant by the 'development gap'?

2 What are Third World countries?

3 What do the initials MEDC and LEDC stand for? What do the terms mean?

4 What is a Fairtrade agreement?

5 List three types of aid.

6 Name three charities which work to provide voluntary aid.

7 What is Agenda 21?

8 How has your community responded to Agenda 21?

An LEDC favela, São Paulo, Brazil

9 Exploring global issues – the human and environmental problems

Researching your topics

Every issue raised and explored in this chapter provides you with a starting point for discussion and debate in the classroom and beyond. You are given the opportunity to formulate and express your opinions on a range of human and environmental global issues. You should research topics carefully so you can present your views in an informed way. Remember that many people will have strong feelings on most of the issues you will study. Try to be honest and express yourself clearly, while being polite and non-offensive. Try to accept the views of others when they do not agree with your own.

Debating global issues

Figure 9.1 From 'A curriculum for global citizenship', Oxfam

The key elements of responsible global citizenship

Knowledge and understanding

- Social justice and equality
- Diversity
- Globalization and interdependence
- Sustainable development
- Peace and conflict

Skills

- Critical thinking
- Ability to argue effectively
- Ability to challenge injustice and inequalities
- Respect for people and things
- Co-operation and conflict resolution

Values and attitudes

- Sense of identity and self-esteem
- Empathy
- Commitment to social justice and equality
- Value and respect for diversity
- Concern for the environment and commitment to sustainable development
- Belief that people can make a difference

As you work through the issues, you should decide whether you agree with the argument given. The writer has made every effort to be free from bias, but there may be issues in which you could question the writer's motives. You should feel free to do so! As a citizen, you have the right to understand fully the systems of which you are a part as a producer, as a consumer, as one of the world's people. Start to ask yourself and other people questions about the issues which affect the world's population and the planet's resources. Below are some examples of questions which you could investigate.

Am I tolerant of other nations and cultures?

Can poverty be prevented?

To make changes and to develop sustainable lifestyles, what needs to happen at local, national and international level?

Are current world trade practices fair? Who gains? Who loses?

Poverty

A basic human right

Everyone has the right to 'a standard of living adequate for health and well-being of themselves and their family, including food, clothing, housing and medical care'. This is the statement made in Article 25 of the UN Universal Declaration of Human Rights. Living in poverty means that people do not have the means to provide these basic needs for themselves and their families.

A 1997 UN Report stated that the poverty in the world had been reduced. But poverty is still a major cause of:

● disease

● poor education

● unnecessary migration

● despair.

These often lead to conflict.

How is poverty measured?

The wealth of a country is measured by how many goods it produces. GNP (Gross National Product) per head of population is normally used to measure a country's development. The GNP is calculated by adding up the values of all the goods and services produced by the country during the year. The total amount is divided by the population to give the GNP per head. The result is given in US dollars to make the comparison between countries easier.

GNP is a reliable measure of wealth in MEDCs. However, many LEDCs do not have correct figures about goods or the population, so the GNP cannot be worked out so accurately.

Other measures of development could be used, for example measuring improvements in health or housing. Another example is the Physical Quality of Life Index. This combines three measures:

● life expectancy (how long people live)

● infant mortality (how many children die)

● literacy (how many people have learnt to read).

Alternative measures of development could include both economic and social factors.

Children living in urban poverty

A global view of poverty

The majority of the world's richest countries are in the northern hemisphere (except for Australia and New Zealand). About 20 per cent of the world's population live in the developed countries. Yet this 20 per cent controls about 80 per cent of the world's wealth. This means that there is an unequal distribution of wealth throughout the world.

In all countries there are people who are very rich and people who are very poor. However, very few people in the developed world live in real or absolute poverty, which means that a person earns and owns almost nothing and that every day is a struggle for survival.

Finance

The World Bank and the IMF

When a bank lends money it makes a loan. It will charge interest on this loan by agreeing an interest rate of a certain percentage with the borrower. The borrower is now in debt. That means the borrower owes the bank the sum of money it borrowed as well as the interest which it will pay every year for the length of the loan. To help a country develop its education system, a bank might agree to lend it £10 million to be paid back over twenty years at an interest rate of 10 per cent. In simple terms, this means that the country will need to pay £1 million interest per year. If the country fails to make the repayments of the loan at the correct time, the amount it owes will increase at the rate of interest (10 per cent). The longer it takes to pay, the more the country will need to pay back and the longer it will be in debt.

To borrow money from the World Bank, a country needs to be a member of the International Monetary Fund (IMF). The World Bank is the main international organization that lends money to finance projects in developing countries. The IMF is responsible for managing the world economy by making sure countries trade with each other. The IMF places conditions on the money loaned by the World Bank. The IMF has based its way of working on the system of free trade, which benefits the powerful Western countries. Some people believe that the time has come to change to a system of fair trade, which will benefit the developing countries.

Third World debt

In the 1970s large profits were made in the oil industry. The profits were put in Western banks. The banks had plenty of money so they loaned it to Africa, Latin America and Asia. Many countries have found it difficult to repay the loans. As a result some African countries are falling deeper and deeper into debt. Indeed some African countries spend more on debt repayments than they spend on education and health combined. Debt repayments do not leave enough money for industrial development. Many people believe that the Western world should do more to write off the debts even though this would reduce their income.

Demonstrating to abolish Third World debt

Human rights abuses

The background

The United Nations Universal Declaration of Human Rights was signed in 1948. Its aim was to protect the human rights of people around the world. In its first section it states that 'All human beings are born free and equal in dignity and rights. They are endowed with reason and conscience, and should act towards one another in a spirit of brotherhood'. The United Nations believes that every human being has rights. These rights include:

- freedom from slavery
- the right to go to political and other meetings and demonstrations
- freedom of movement.

The UN Commission on Human Rights was set up to monitor the declaration's operation. It monitors countries for human rights abuse relating to:

- imprisonment
- torture
- the death penalty
- sexual and racial discrimination.

If there is evidence of human rights abuses, the United Nations Council will decide whether to take action against the offending country. This may involve economic sanctions, observers in the country or, rarely, military action.

Non-government organizations

Non-government organizations (NGOs) help the United Nations Commission and other UN bodies with their work. These NGOs include Amnesty International and ACT (Action by Christians against Torture). In some parts of the world people are having their freedoms and even their lives taken away simply because they think differently from their government and speak against government policies. When these people are imprisoned they are known as prisoners of conscience.

Amnesty International was founded in 1961. It investigates and tries to stop human rights abuses. Amnesty International has over 1 million members in 150 countries. It is the world's largest voluntary organization working to protect human rights.

It aims to make sure that:

- all prisoners of conscience are released

- all political prisoners have a fair and prompt trial

- torture and the death penalty are stopped.

What are human rights abuses?

There are many examples in the world today of human rights abuses. Perhaps the most obvious abuse is that more than 1 billion people are living in extreme poverty. Human rights are abused in many areas of life, for example when people:

- are not allowed freedom of speech

- are not allowed the freedom to practise a religion of their choice either in public or in private

- are tortured

- are not given the right to a fair trial

- are discriminated against on the grounds of race, disability, sex or religion

- are denied a basic standard of living.

Some groups would argue that not allowing people the right to die (euthanasia) is a human rights abuse. Euthanasia is not allowed under British law, but it is allowed in some other countries.

A boy weaving carpets in India

The rights of the child

Children are more likely to be abused than any other group in society. In 1989 the UN produced the Declaration of the Rights of the Child. This sets out the rights of the child with respect to:

- survival – children should have a decent standard of living and good health

- development – children have the right to a full and free education

- protection – children have the right to be protected from slavery, exploitation, cruelty or enforced separation from their family

- participation – children have the right to express an opinion on any issue that effects them, including their health and education.

There is still much to be done to meet the aims of this declaration. For example, in some countries children work long hours and are poorly paid. It is estimated that 17.5 million children under the age of fourteen work for a small amount of money in India.

The issue of arms and weapons

The background

The world spends more on arms than on anything else. Developing countries buy over half the world's arms. They spend 66 per cent more on military strength than on education.

Biological and chemical weapons can kill large numbers of people. Biological weapons include the use of viruses and bacteria which cause death in humans. Chemical weapons include toxic substances which will kill or disable people or poison food or water supplies.

The arms trade

The arms trade describes the manufacture and sale of a wide range of military weapons, vehicles and equipment. It refers to items such as fighter aircraft, tanks, missiles, guns and grenades. The British Government is one agency that sells arms. The government might offer aid to a developing country so it can build roads. In return the country might buy arms from Britain. If the country finds it difficult to pay the agreed amount for the arms, the debt is sometimes cancelled.

One result of the arms trade can be an arms race. This happens when one country buys military equipment and neighbouring countries feel threatened so they buy arms too. Countries then compete against each other to make sure they have enough weapons.

Nuclear weapons

Nuclear weapons were first developed by the USA during World War II (1939–45). Only two nuclear bombs have ever been dropped in populated areas. This happened in 1945 when the USA dropped bombs on the cities of Hiroshima and Nagasaki in Japan.

There has been a big increase in the number of countries that have nuclear missiles. One reason for the increase is that improved technology has made it cheaper for countries to develop nuclear missiles. Supporters of nuclear weapons argue that they are necessary to protect the country and prevent war. Critics say that the huge amount of money spent on nuclear weapons (one missile costs $12 million) could be spent on the environment and overseas aid instead.

Hiroshima, after the nuclear bomb was dropped, 1945

Landmines

A landmine is a small bomb which is buried under, on, or near the ground. It is designed to explode when a weight, usually a person or a vehicle, passes near to it or over it. There are many places in the world where landmines, which were used in times of conflict, have been left in the ground. These landmines continue to cause injury and death to the local residents. Over 10 000 people are killed each year by landmines, while 16 000 are injured. Removing landmines is expensive and takes time. For every 5000 landmines removed, one skilled person will be killed and two people will be injured.

International law makes it clear that in times of war and conflict civilians should be protected as far as possible and never directly attacked. However, landmines are still used widely. The 1999 Ottawa Treaty banned the use of landmines. By 2000, 89 countries had signed the treaty. However, one developed country, the USA, refused to sign the treaty.

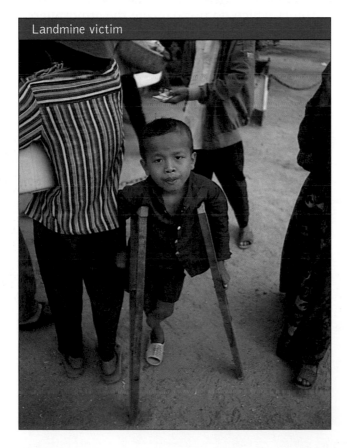
Landmine victim

Global warming

The background

Global warming is not new. The world has seen many changes in temperature during its 4600-million-year history. These changes have taken place naturally over a period of time. What is worrying scientists today is the speed at which change is taking place and the way people's actions are accelerating the changes. As a result of climate change, droughts, floods and hurricanes have affected places that are not used to such extreme weather conditions. Global warming is causing ice sheets to melt and sea levels to rise. This will cause flooding in low-lying coastal areas.

How does it happen?

If there is too much carbon in the atmosphere, more heat from the Earth's surface is trapped. This is known as the greenhouse effect. Greenhouse gases, such as methane, water vapour and nitrogen oxides, trap the heat from the sun in the atmosphere and the result is global warming. An increase in any of these gases will make the global temperature rise and can cause a hole to form in the Earth's protective ozone layer. These holes in the ozone layer mean more heat from the sun reaches the Earth.

Some factors affecting global warming

- Heat from the sun in the form of radiation passes through the atmosphere and warms the land and sea.

- Carbon dioxide traps the heat reflected back from the Earth. As more carbon dioxide is produced, more heat is trapped.

- CFCs from aerosols and refrigeration plants trap heat in the atmosphere and thin the ozone layer.

- Carbon dioxide comes from burning forests and rotting trees.

- Waste from both people and animals produces the greenhouse gas methane.

- Burning coal, gas and oil adds carbon to the atmosphere. This carbon traps heat.

- The number of vehicles in the world is growing. Oil and petrol exhaust causes greenhouse gases.

- The use of fertilizers which are nitrogen based adds more nitrous oxide to the atmosphere.

- The oceans and seas absorb carbon dioxide from the atmosphere, but we now produce more than the oceans can absorb, so it stays in the air.

What needs to be done?

Environmentalists argue that we need to cut the amount of energy we use. This would reduce the amount of greenhouse gases we produce and so slow down the rate of global warming. This could be done by:

- using less energy in our homes and workplaces, for example by increasing insulation and using low-energy light bulbs

- increasing the amount of materials we use that can be recycled

- walking to local shops for our weekly shopping and using public transport instead of private cars for longer journeys.

Friends of the Earth and Greenpeace say that using less energy is not enough. They say that we need to develop the use of renewable energy sources such as solar panels and wind turbines which do not damage the atmosphere by producing greenhouse gases.

A wind farm – a renewable energy source

Acid rain

The background

Rain is always slightly acidic as carbon dioxide is dissolved as the drops of rain fall through the atmosphere. Such acidity is strong enough to dissolve limestone and change the shape of the rock. In Europe and North America the rain is sometimes one hundred times more acid than the rain which causes rocks to erode. This is because the rain is polluted.

Burning coal, gas and oil, and exhaust from cars releases sulphur dioxide and nitrogen oxides into the atmosphere, where they dissolve in the water droplets in the clouds. The pollutants then become part of the water cycle and the result is acid rain.

The wind can carry the water droplets for great distances before they fall as rain or snow.

Scientists have warned that global warming is likely to increase acid rain in the future, as higher temperatures can increase the rate of chemical changes.

The effects of acid rain

In New York State, USA, almost 6 per cent of all the lakes and ponds are badly affected by acid rain. Local people report the loss of fish, birds, otters and other animals from the lakes. Acid rain is also causing trees to die, particularly in Europe and North America.

Acid rain can damage buildings, statues and bridges. Buildings made of limestone are particularly at risk. If left untreated, bridges may pose a safety risk, and castles and cathedrals are at risk of crumbling.

Acid rain can have a direct effect on people's health. It can cause breathing problems, coughs and headaches. Poisonous chemicals from the rain can be stored in fruit, vegetables and animals, making food a danger to people.

The effects of acid rain in plain view

What can be done?

Acid rain can be reduced, but all countries in the world will have to make an agreement and keep to it. It will be costly to put in place. Acid rain can be reduced by:

- cutting the amount of sulphur dioxide given off by power stations by burning low sulphur coal or alternative fuels

- cutting harmful exhausts from cars by improving car engines and using cleaner fuels

- using energy sources such as hydro-electric power and wind, solar and tidal power

- having an international agreement backed by laws and finance in each country

- informing the public and changing people's habits with respect to saving energy, for example turning off lights, insulating houses, using cars less.

Deforestation

The background

In 1990, 1.7 billion cubic metres of wood and paper were used worldwide. It is predicted that this will have increased by 60 per cent by the year 2010. Across the world, forests are being cut down or made into huge plantations to meet the demand for newspapers, writing paper, doors and window frames, wooden flooring and junk mail. By taking this wood from the world's forests, we threaten the existence of hundreds of plant and animal species and we change the way of life for millions of forest people.

The causes of deforestation

The main cause of deforestation is simply the cutting down of trees (see Figure 9.2).

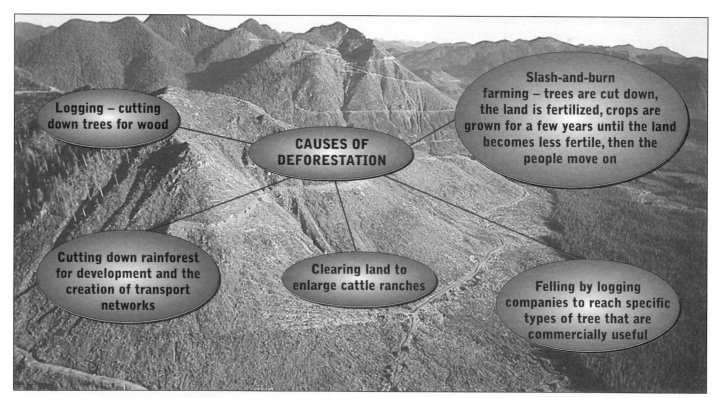

Figure 9.2 The causes of deforestation

Rainforests have been destroyed in Brazil, Colombia, Indonesia, Thailand, Mexico and Nigeria. As these countries are faced by the problems of Third World debt, over-population, war, famine or floods, the governments of these countries argue that they have no alternative. They want their countries to develop, and the only way they can make use of their countries' natural resources is through deforestation.

Why save the rainforests?

The rainforests cover only 2 per cent of the world's surface, but they are the oldest and the richest of the world's ecosystems (see page 146). They:

- contain 50 per cent of all the world's living species

South American rainforest – a river of destruction

- provide plants from which medicines are made
- are the home of many local peoples
- prevent soil erosion because tree roots anchor the soil
- control the balance of gases in the atmosphere, reducing the greenhouse effect
- prevent flooding and maintain moisture levels in the atmosphere
- protect soils from sunlight because only 1 per cent of solar radiation can pass through the canopy of the forest.

The threat to coniferous forests

Conifers are extremely important for the supply of wood and timber. There are major timber industries in Scandinavia, Canada and Russia. When trees are cut down in coniferous forests, they are usually replaced. But the replacement plantations are not natural ecosystems. They support fewer species of plants and animals than the natural forests. In June 2000 Greenpeace gave evidence on its website of illegal logging activities in Russia. This is a common problem in Russia and there are currently no punishments.

Sustainable forestry

One way to repair the damage caused by deforestation is sustainable forestry. This is practised by the Forestry Commission in Scotland. It means that for every tree that is felled, another is planted in its place. Environmentalists argue that it is necessary to plant extra trees to make up for all the trees that were cut down in the past.

Protecting the world's ecosystems

What are ecosystems?

In any environment there are rocks and soils, plants, animals, people, water, the atmosphere and climate. The relationship between all of these and the effect they have on each other is described as an ecosystem. An ecosystem can be at any scale, from a small pond on a farm to tropical rainforests.

How do ecosystems work?

An ecosystem is a cycle of activity (Figure 9.3). The sunlight is taken in by plants and passed through the system as food for insects and animals. Other animals eat these insects and animals. The plants, insects and animals act as temporary stores of energy. Eventually the plants and animals die. As they rot they provide nutrients such as nitrogen and calcium for the soil. These nutrients are then taken in through the roots of plants and are used to feed the plants. The cycle starts again.

Ecosystems and biodiversity

We rely on our environment to meet our needs. It seems sensible that we should look after our environment for future generations to use as we have used it. This means that we should manage the environment so that a wide variety of wildlife and ecosystems continues to exist. This variety of systems is known as biodiversity.

Managing the world's ecosystems

Ecosystem management is becoming increasingly important. Many ecosystems have been targeted for conservation. These are known as World Heritage Areas. One World Heritage Area is the Galapagos Islands, off the coast of Ecuador. This is an ideal site for conservationists to protect and study. However, the unique wildlife and the exciting volcanic peaks make it a tourist attraction. There is conflict between conservation and development efforts. Even though the number of tourists allowed to visit the islands is kept to a minimum, people worry that the ecosystem is under threat. Future decisions on the environment should allow for human use while protecting the natural ecosystems.

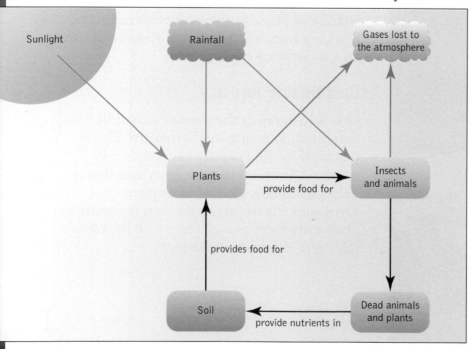

Figure 9.3 A simple ecosystem

What are you going to do about it?

We are beginning to realize that our habits and actions affect the balance of the planet and, consequently, the lives of millions of people in other countries. The wealthiest countries in the world are the biggest users of energy, minerals and food. Now, we must come to terms with what we have done to the planet. The young people of today are the decision-makers of tomorrow. It will be up to you to change things and increase the Earth's chances of survival. There is much to be done. Every action, no matter how small, will help. This page provides some ideas for you.

It will be up to the young people of today to save the planet for future generations. So don't just sit there – do something!

Join a local group and help in the community.

Write to your MP or local councillor to tell them what you think should be done.

Support some of the organizations mentioned in the book. You could write to tell them you support them or raise money for their efforts.

(Remember that these organizations are charities, so if you want a reply enclose an s.a.e.)

Encourage your school, youth club or other group to link with a Third World community.

Use pump sprays or CFC-free aerosols.

Join a national or international group and get involved in their activities. (Make sure that your parents have given permission, as there is usually a cost to join such organizations.)

Save water – turn the tap off when you clean your teeth!

Start recycling glass bottles, aluminium cans and paper.

Save electricity – switch off the lights when they are not needed and don't overfill the kettle!

Buy recycled paper products.

Re-use your plastic bags.

Walk to school.

Check it out

What you should have learned from this chapter

Look at the areas of study in the table. You should now know and understand the language and ideas that we have explored in Chapter 9: Exploring global issues.

The activities and questions in the chapter, and the worksheets your teacher will have worked through with you, should have helped you to learn about this topic.

If some of the areas are not clear, read through the pages again. If you are still not sure then ask your teacher to explain them again.

Area of study	Page
Poverty	136
Finance	137
Human rights abuses	138
The rights of the child	139
Arms and weapons	140
Global warming	141
Acid rain	143
Deforestation and ecosystems	144, 146
Making changes – What will you do?	147

You should be able to answer all the following questions. These are short answer questions similar to those that will appear in Section A of the written exam paper that you will sit at the end of the course.

The knowledge and ideas covered in this chapter will also be tested in longer, more detailed questions in Sections B and D of the exam paper.

1 How is the wealth of a country measured?

2 Where are most of the world's richest countries?

3 What does IMF stand for?

4 What is the World Bank?

5 Name two NGOs which work to prevent human rights abuse.

6 What is the UN Universal Declaration of Human Rights?

7 When have nuclear weapons been used in war?

8 List three ways we can all help to reduce global warming.

9 Give two effects of acid rain.

10 What is an ecosystem?

11 What is the main cause of deforestation?

12 Name four countries where rainforests are being destroyed.

Coursework and exam techniques

Key ideas

Days of exams are hard — but they can really broaden your horizons . . .

10 Coursework

There are two parts to the GCSE exam in Citizenship Studies:

- coursework, which carries 40 per cent of the marks
- written exam paper, which carries 60 per cent of the marks.

Both parts are important.

What is coursework?

The purpose of the coursework is for you to take responsibility and take part in a citizenship activity. It may be an activity within your school or in the wider community. No one else can do this for you – it must be your own work. The grade you finally achieve will depend on your own effort and commitment. This does not mean that you are on your own – your teacher will offer you all the help and guidance possible.

What do you need to do?

You may be given a choice of activities to choose from, or your group may all work together on one activity. Your teacher will make sure the activity you are involved in is suitable. You must be able to show that you have:

- planned the activity
- taken part in the activity
- found some information

- written up an account of what you and others did
- evaluated what you did.

All this will be done in stages. Make sure you keep up to date with your work at each stage.

Assessment

The coursework must provide evidence that:

- you have taken part in a citizenship activity
- you understand why the activity is suitable
- you have found and used information
- you have been able to express opinions about what you have found.

In evaluating the activity you must show the part you have played and the opinions and contributions of other people.

The coursework is marked by your teacher and may be sent to a moderator, who will make sure that standards of marking are the same from all schools. Teachers and moderators work to the same mark scheme, which is divided into four sections:

- planning (10 marks)
- knowledge and understanding of events and roles (10 marks)
- explanation and interpretation of evidence (15 marks)
- evaluation (15 marks).

Another 3 marks can be given for how well you put across your ideas, making a possible total of 53 marks.

Carrying out the coursework

Stage 1 Planning

Once you have determined the activity you are to carry out, you must start to plan it.

In your written work you will need to:

- give a very clear description of what you are going to do (the aims of the activity)

- show why you are doing it

- show how it relates to the course

- show who it will help or who will benefit.

The plan you are about to produce is often called an action plan.

Write down some ideas. Read them again and give the plan a structure including all the necessary details of what you need to do in the right order. Think about the best way of presenting your action plan. You could use a flow chart for the initial ideas (make sure you include it in your final presentation), then work out a more detailed chart showing:

- the order of events

- who will be involved

- when the different events are to take place

- what resources you will need

- if possible, some idea of the timing of events

- what you need to find out, i.e. what research you will need to do.

Your teacher may provide you with a chart to complete, or you may draw one yourself. You may use computers to help you to present your work if you like, but this is not essential.

Good, thoughtful planning is essential for success. Consider very carefully what you are going to do and write the plan in as much detail as you can. Try to think of everything – and if your teacher makes helpful suggestions about things you have left out, be sure to include them in your plan.

Stage 2 Account of the activity

Now your plan is approved and complete, put the plan into action.

Do your research thoroughly. Consider the presentation of your coursework carefully. If you need to change the action plan because of what you find out, that's fine. Write up what you are changing and why – you get marks for being able to make changes and give reasons for them.

While you are involved in the activity you will get to know people quite well in a variety of situations or roles. If the activity is carried out during a short space of time, as soon as it is over it is best to write down your thoughts and reactions to what you did, what others did, how they felt, other people's opinions, and your own feelings and opinions.

If the activity is going to continue over a period of time, it would be sensible to keep a diary of important events or situations. This could include comments on:

- what happened

- who was involved

- how you felt at the time

- how others were affected.

Now that you have planned, researched and carried out the activity, you have to write an account of all that you have done. The marks for this account are awarded in two ways:

- how you show your knowledge and understanding of the events that took place and the roles and relationships of all the people who were involved. There is a total of 10 marks for this. Look at your notes or diary. Think about what happened, the part you played and the part other people played. Ask what your responsibilities were and what other people's were.

- how you explain and interpret evidence. There is a total of 15 marks for this. You must show that you understand the purpose of the activity and present all the information you have found out. Include any regional, national or global links. Analyse the evidence you have collected and present it in a variety of ways. If you can, include a chart, picture, photograph or diagram, to explain the information or data. Write about your opinions based on the evidence you have presented. Mention any current issues surrounding the activity – write about these to show your knowledge.

The write-up

Try to include as many points from the advice above as you can. Gather all the data/information/diary entries/notes that you have for the activity. Think about the order you are going to present it in and the methods of presentation you are going to use. Show that you are able to organize and present information clearly, and that you are able to express your opinions.

Start by setting the scene:

- describe the purpose of the activity
- describe where the activity took place
- if the activity is related to a local or regional issue, write about the issue.

Then write about the activity:

- write about your part in the activity and the people you met
- write about some of the important ideas you have learned about, such as the rights, roles and responsibilities of all those involved including yourself
- think about questions such as:
  - How did you get on with other people?
  - Were they the same age or much older than you?
  - How were you treated?

Write up your thoughts about these.

- Include any written comments from those responsible for the activity or from other pupils you worked with about:

- the activity and your part in it and theirs
- how you worked
- your attitude towards the activity and other people involved.

To finish the report:

- form your own opinions from the work you have presented and state these opinions
- draw conclusions from all that happened during the activity and write them down.

Stage 3: Evaluation

The evaluation is an important section and is worth 15 marks. An evaluation is a critical look at all that went on throughout the activity.

You need to show:

- why the activity was suitable – you must show that you knew the purpose of what you were involved in
- the things you did and what was good or not so good about each
- how well your action plan worked, any changes that were made and why the changes were necessary
- your understanding of your own contribution as well as that of others – stating how well people worked together
- the rights, roles and responsibilities of all the people involved
- any problems you came across and how they were solved – who suggested the solutions to problems
- what you and others learned from the activity
- who benefited from the activity and how
- what was achieved overall
- suggestions for any improvements that could be made if a similar activity was to be repeated.

You need to show that you took an active part in and made a valuable contribution to the event.

Remember to read your work through thoroughly before you hand it in, and make corrections where needed.

A final point

Now put the finishing touches to your report. Make an attractive front cover stating the following:

- the name of your school/centre

- the centre number

- your name

- your candidate number

- the course – GCSE Citizenship Studies

- the title of your report.

Add one final page at the back for acknowledgements (list the people who helped you) and a bibliography (list any books, magazines, leaflets, websites, etc. from which you obtained information).

11 Exam techniques

There is only one written paper for this course (there are no higher or foundation tiers). It carries 60 per cent of the marks towards your exam grade.

There are no short cuts, only you can learn the work. Make yourself a revision plan. Set yourself targets and give yourself rewards when you achieve them. Everyone learns in a different way. By now you should know what suits you best.

The question paper

The question paper is divided into four sections: A, B, C and D. Each section is different, therefore different types of answers are required.

The exam paper will be in booklet form. You will need to put your details on the front cover and answer the questions in the booklet. Read the instructions at the beginning of each section and follow them carefully. You will have one and a half hours (90 minutes) to complete the paper.

Section A

You must answer all the questions in this section. The questions are straightforward and need short, factual answers. If you have been answering the questions at the end of each chapter, you should be familiar with this type of question (go back through these and test your knowledge).

The questions will cover all areas in all of the Topics.

Section B

In this section you must answer one compulsory source-based question. The question will be divided into different parts. You must answer all parts of the question.

You will be given a short piece of text to read containing information about a situation. You will then be asked a question about the passage you have read, which will mean you have to make a judgement to show your understanding of it.

Another part of the question will ask you to use the information given and combine it with your own knowledge, for example on a community, a business or a world issue. You will be asked to write an answer or say what a possible outcome might be.

In a further part of the question you will need to add your knowledge, form an opinion or describe who could influence the situation and how.

Section C

This section will contain one compulsory question divided into different parts. All parts of the question will relate to the citizenship activity you have taken part in for your coursework. You will be asked about your part in the activity. You must answer all parts of the question.

This should be an easier section, as you should know more than anyone else about what you did.

Possible information you will be asked to provide includes:

- a good description or outline of your citizenship activity

- an outline of how you planned the activity – think about any changes you made and your reasons for the changes, and include these in the evaluation

- what your contribution was and your opinions on the activity

- contributions made by others and what their opinions were

- your thoughts on how successful it was, who benefited from the activity, and who learned what

- how the activity could have been improved.

You could prepare answers to these questions as part of your revision. You will then know the answers very well before the exam.

Note:
Read through your report on the activity as part of your exam revision.

Section D

In this section you will be asked to write an essay. You must choose one title from a choice of three.

All the essay titles will be from the themes that run throughout the course:

- rights and responsibilities

- decision-making, power and authority

- participation in citizenship activities.

Guidance will be given about what you should include in your answer. These are not the only areas to cover, but you should include all those mentioned in the guidance and also use your own knowledge of the subject.

Read all the essay titles and the suggested topics to include and make sure you understand what each one is asking. Now decide which one to tackle. Take a minute or two to think about your answer and what order you will put the topics in. Make a brief outline of the essay including what to put into each paragraph.

Now write the essay, remembering to give reasons for any judgements you make. Present the facts and well-reasoned arguments, then state your opinion, which should be based on what you have written in the answer.

A final word

Plan your time wisely. Each section is worth the same number of marks, so make sure you complete all parts of each section. When you have finished the paper, go back to the beginning and read each answer carefully, completing any parts that you have missed out. Check spelling and punctuation as a possible 6 marks for this will be added to your total.

Whatever grade you achieve in Citizenship Studies, studying this course will have made you a more informed citizen. **Good luck!**

Glossary

Acid rain Rain contaminated by chemicals from burning fuels

Advertising Techniques used to persuade consumers to buy goods

Agenda 21 Action plan for sustainable development agreed at Rio Summit (1992)

Aid programmes Transfer of money, goods and expertise from one country to another

Authority A form of power accepted as a legal right to rule

Budget Economic statement about taxation and spending targets

Civil law Relates to people's private rights, such as boundaries and marital breakdown

Commonwealth A group of nations, many of which were formerly British colonies

Community All the people who live or work in an area

Consumer Person buying goods or services

Contract of employment Written document containing terms and conditions of employment

Crime Any illegal or unlawful act against property or people

Criminal law Relates to crimes against people or property

Culture Shared language, behaviour, traditions and values of a society

Deforestation Felling trees to make wood and paper products

Development gap Divide between the two-thirds of the world's population who live in poverty and the other third who live in plenty

Devolution Transfer or delegation of power to regional level

Discrimination Treating people less favourably than others because of their gender, ethnicity, religion, culture or disability

Economy How goods, services and finances are provided and managed

Ecosystem Relationship between rocks, soils, vegetation, living organisms, water, atmosphere and climate

Equal opportunities Fair treatment without discrimination for everyone

Ethnic identity Particular culture of a group within society

European Convention on Human Rights (ECHR) Identifies citizens' human rights

European Union (EU) group of 15 states trading labour, goods and services in single market

Fairtrade Trade organizations giving workers a reasonable price for their goods and labour

Finance Money raised for development through taxation or borrowing

Free trade Use of low-priced raw materials and labour to create profit for multinational companies and countries

Freedom of speech The idea that people should be able to air their opinions without punishment

Global warming Climate change caused by industrial and domestic gases which destroy the protective ozone layer and expose the Earth to increased heat

Government Democratically elected members of parliament who set taxes to pay for public services and make laws for everyone to live by

Health and safety at work Responsibilities of employers and employees to ensure safe working practices

Human rights basic entitlements to liberty, justice, privacy, education and freedom

Industry Businesses involving raw materials/natural resources to manufacture products, or services

Law-making Parliamentary process for designing new laws

Local government System of councils responsible for looking after people, services and facilities in a country or urban area

Media Newspapers, books and magazines, radio, television and video, advertising, cinema and the Internet

Multinational company Any free-trade business operating in several countries to keep costs low and profits high

North Atlantic Treaty Organization (NATO) Alliance of 19 countries committed to each others' defence

Political party People sharing the same views who fight elections to form a government

Poverty Insufficient food, clothing, housing, water, sanitation and medical care

Power The ability to influence or to rule

Pressure group People who join together to influence or change government policy

Racism Treating people less favourably because they are from a different race

Religion System of values and beliefs

Responsibilities Duties towards oneself and others

Rights Freedoms to which one is entitled

School community A number of people working and learning together, sharing the same values and rules

Sustainable development Meeting the needs of the present without compromising the needs of the future

Taxation Money taken from citizens by the government to finance public services

Third World Countries with poor living standards, high birth and death rates, high infant mortality and low life expectancy

Trade Any system for buying and selling goods and services

Trade union Collection of workers who join together to promote their common interests

United Nations (UN) Organization set up after World War II to promote international peace, security and co-operation

Voluntary organisations Support groups who raise funds for and awareness of specific community issues or special groups

Voting Citizens' opportunity to decide who should govern them

World Trade Organization (WTO) Free trade organization regulating import and export of goods between countries

Index